*Jake Stahl has done what very few can. He's built a blueprint for communication that actually works in the real world. Own the Room isn't another book of scripts or clichés. It's a playbook for becoming unforgettable, for showing up in a way that makes people lean in and listen. I've seen Jake's work up close, and he doesn't just talk about presence, he creates it. If you've ever been overlooked, dismissed, or talked over, this book is the reset button you've been waiting for.*

—Steve Carlis, Award Winning Media Executive; Co-Founder 2MM Media Partnership Group

*If you've ever struggled to explain the real value of what you do or watched a prospect nod along without actually getting it, the STRATA framework will hit home. Jake Stahl doesn't just give you another framework. He gives you language that lands, stories that stick, and a structure that actually helps people see the cost of doing nothing. I've used a lot of tools, strategies and tactics in sales. This one is at the top. If you want to be the best, you have to learn from the best—which Jake is!*

—Bryan McDonald, Partner at onPurpose Growth, Keynote Speaker

In Own the Room, *Jake Stahl delivers a communication manual that is as raw and personal as it is practical. At its core lies STRATA, a six-part framework designed to move beyond rehearsed pitches into real influence built on presence, awareness, and alignment. What makes this book stand out is its origin story. Stahl doesn't write from a pedestal; he writes from rock bottom. His journey through addiction and reinvention gives this book a lived authenticity. Each chapter blends stories with step-by-step techniques, showing how subtle human signals can shift outcomes. Verdict: A powerful, practical, and deeply human guide to communication that earns a place alongside the classics of influence and leadership.*

—Devin Sizemore, Best-Selling Author of *Connection Expansion*, Host of ACES Connection Group, and Super Connector

*I buy a lot of books. Most become coasters. This one didn't. It rewired what I notice in the first five seconds. I used to enter rooms trying to prove I was right, then wondered why nothing ever moved past "interesting." This book taught me how to be read right, spot the tells, and give ideas back so people owned them with less effort, more movement. Tired of stalled conversations? Use one idea in your next pitch, call, or 1:1. You'll feel the difference immediately.*

—Julie Diekman, CEO of Limitless Ideation, Creator of The First 30 Fix

Own the Room *by Jake Stahl isn't your typical communication or sales book. It's raw, personal, and practical. At the heart is Stahl's STRATA framework, refined with countless clients.... and it works. What makes it powerful is how it moves beyond words, breaking down the unspoken signals, posture, tone, and presence that shape every interaction. The beauty is its versatility: just as relevant to parenting and relationships as it is to closing deals or leading teams. If you've ever walked away from a conversation thinking, "Why didn't that land?" this book shows you why.... and what to do differently. Highly recommend.*

—Jon Goehring, Founder of StoryTrust Media, Award Winning Podcaster and Radio Host

*Jake Stahl's STRATA has cracked the code on real-time interpersonal intelligence, and it couldn't have come at a better moment in my career. As someone who leans introverted and has often felt out of place in sales, this framework resonates because it's something I can actually practice and apply. One of my biggest takeaways: stop chasing a simple "yes" and instead create a shared space where agreement naturally emerges. Grounded in neuroscience, STRATA feels fresh and authentic, not forced. Its power extends beyond business into social and family life. For anyone wanting to own the room without losing their authentic self, this is a true game changer.*

—Cory Hanscom, Founder, Brand Articulate

Own the Room *by Jake Stahl isn't just another communication book. It's a survival guide for anyone who's ever felt invisible despite saying all the right things. Jake's story, from addiction and loss to mastering presence, gives this book raw authenticity. STRATA isn't just an acronym; it's a lifeline. What makes this powerful is how Jake teaches you to read the room—posture, tone, rhythm, presence, and subtle triggers most people miss—and to adjust without forcing. Whether closing deals, leading teams, or connecting at home, the skill changes everything. Practical, tested, and deeply human, this book shows how genuine presence wins every time.*

—Rick Maher, CEO and Visionary of Turning Point
HCM, A Fractional HR Firm

*People don't just hear your words. They feel them. With powerful examples and hands-on exercises, Jake Stahl shows why tone and presence can make or break your message. If you're ready to transform the way you connect, influence, and lead,* Own the Room *is your playbook for truly impactful communication.*

—Dave Jacobson, Sales Coach, Jacobson Coaching
Leadership

*I love* Own the Room *because it digs deeply into the psychology and emotional pulls that make people move forward, or away, and shows how to improve our own approaches to leverage this insight. Jake Stahl tells some very uncomfortable truths about why we don't achieve the results we want, and they have nothing to do with intelligence, preparation, or certifications. These truths, if faced and applied through STRATA, transform not only results but also the respect and credibility we earn with clients, colleagues, and relationships. I had a hard time stopping myself from highlighting every sentence.*

—Nancy Fox, CEO of WYZE Rainmakers, author of top book on networking, *Network Like a Fox: A Targeted Approach to Building Successful Business Relationships in Person and Online*

*Jake Stahl doesn't just write about sales—he shares what it means to hit rock bottom, rebuild from nothing, and come back stronger. His story is ultimately about how we send, receive, and respond to signals. This is less a business development manual and more a guide to building authentic relationships. You'll walk away with practical insights for communicating more effectively, whether you're in a boardroom, a client pitch, or a personal conversation. And in an age where AI can generate words but not authenticity, this book makes a compelling case for why human connection remains the ultimate advantage. A must-read.*

—Lucas Blondheim, Founder & Principal Product Designer, Fennec Design Studio

*Jake Stahl's courage and vulnerability in sharing his story of addiction and recovery—and the privilege of co-founding Orchestraight with him—have revealed a man at the top of his craft. STRATA is his seminal work, and it's a book I finally feel ready to read. When I met Jake, he saw something in me that connected us deeply. For someone like me—recently diagnosed with ADHD and often struggling to feel understood—Jake's way of making communication accessible and empowering is extraordinary. Whether you want to sell, lead, or simply be a better husband, father, or friend, his approach elevates you. This is next-level work.*

—Russell Fette, Founder & Managing Partner of Financial Rhythms, Creator of Financial Rhythm System™

*STRATA works because you can practice it, and benefit from it, every day. Some of us may be professional salespeople, but the truth is, we're all negotiators. More importantly, we're all trying to connect with others, and with ourselves. And, in many ways, our happiness depends on how well we audition for life's moments of truth. That's why Jake Stahl's hard-earned STRATA framework isn't just for business. It's for everyone. We're fortunate that the book is as readable as it is: high energy, full of practical specifics, and most importantly, filled with opportunities to practice what you learn.*

—Clark Aldrich, award-winning designer and author of *Unschooling Rules* and *Short Sims*, recognized by *Fortune* and *CNN* as one of the world's leading voices in experiential learning.

*If you've ever felt a conversation shift and wondered what you missed, this book is for you. Jake Stahl teaches you to master the art of reading subtle signals and pivoting in real time—so you meet the room that's actually there, not the one in your head. Once you can see the tells and adjust with intention, the way you enter every conversation changes. Clear, practical moves you'll use every day, in business and in life.*

—Mary Kate O'Connell, Executive Coach and
Entrepreneur

*Most books on communication are safe. This one isn't. Jake Stahl strips away the fluff and gives you what actually works when the room is stacked against you. STRATA isn't theory, it's a weapon. I've watched Jake take people who were invisible and make them undeniable. If you're done blending in, this is the book that finally shows you how to be unforgettable without being fake.*

—Hank Norman, Media Coach to Global Brands &
Co-Founder of 2MM Media Partnership Group

*STRATA is a game-changer. Jake Stahl provides a powerful and practical system for decoding the 'conversation beneath the conversation.' If you want to move from being simply heard to being felt and remembered, this book is your new playbook. An essential read for any leader.*

—Brian Lofrumento, Founder & CEO, Ops+AI, Host
of Top 1% podcast, Wantrepreneur to Entrepreneur,
President of Board of Director for non-profit Through
Entrepreneurship

*Formulating and delivering a message that truly lands is tricky. A pro ball player might have a better chance of hitting a home run than most of us do connecting with a client or prospect. We're asked to project confidence without arrogance, vulnerability without weakness, and passion without self-absorption. In this book, Stahl reveals the human-perception design of STRATA through vivid, real-world examples. Applying his tools will elevate how you listen, perceive, and communicate—and dramatically improve your business batting average. If you want to master live communication and unlock the dynamics behind real connection, this is the playbook.*

—Lori Crever, corporate communications specialist, comedy improvisor, and author of *Protégé Power: A Roadmap to Mentorship*

# OWN

## THE

# ROOM

# OWN

## THE

# ROOM

How to Communicate to Be Seen,
Heard and Respected

JAKE STAHL

THIN LEAF PRESS | LOS ANGELES

Library of Congress Cataloging-in-Publication Data
Names: Stahl, Jake, Author
Title: *Own the Room: How to Communicate to Be Seen, Heard and Respected*
LCCN: On File

ISBN 978-1-968318-24-6 (hardcover) | 978-1-968318-25-3 (paperback)
ISBN 978-1-968318-24-6 (eBook)

Business, Communication, Interpersonal Relations, Personal Growth
Cover Design: 100 Covers
Interior Design: Dindo Sanguenza
Editor: Erik Seversen
Thin Leaf Press
Los Angeles

THIN
LEAF

For my wife—who never stopped believing in who I could become.

For my kids—who remind me every day that showing up matters more than being perfect.

And for those I hurt, those who helped, and those who never gave up on me.

You're the reason this story didn't end where it began.

# FOREWORD

By Erik Seversen

As I sit in my office writing, I'm surrounded by books. Literally. Three of the four walls are filled floor-to-ceiling with books, and I've read most of them. I am one of those who think that books can change lives. As I reflect on some of the influential books surrounding me, I think of Dale Carnegie, Napoleon Hill, Stephen Covey, Zig Ziglar, Simon Sinek, Tony Robbins, and many more. I feel overwhelmed by the knowledge I've gained from these people. However, I've also read quite a few books that didn't meet the mark. I've either put them down unfinished or more commonly finished them, hoping to gain something, and quickly forgot them.

Having read hundreds of books on professional development, it is clear to me which books have had the largest impact on me and one common thread is that each of these books had some formula to follow that would help me in some way. Zig Ziglar's formula was to find success by helping others find their success; Napoleon Hill's formula was to imagine what you wanted so that it *could* become a reality, Stephen Covey's formula was a system aimed at providing you with influence; Simon Sinek's formula was to put the *why* before the *how* and the *what*. You get the picture. Well, I'm happy to say that I was recently introduced to a book that has a precise formula about a topic that I find fundamentally important to success—communication. The book is called *Own the Room: How to Communicate to Be Seen, Heard and Respected* and happily you are holding it now.

*Own the Room* was written by Jake Stahl. I first met Jake as we co-authored a book together and from the first moment I met him to well after our book was published, I was always impressed with the conversations with Jake. They were always meaningful and I felt good after them. I didn't know it then but this isn't just because Jake is a charming guy. It is because Jake was very intentional in all of our communication, and he was actually using strategies that made me feel important, made my ideas feel valuable, and made me want to work with him. Jake was using a communication style which he has coined STRATA, an acronym you'll learn a lot about in this book.

STRATA wasn't born from Jake sitting down and brainstorming how to communicate better. STRATA was born from Jake's battle with opioid addiction, when he burned a lot of bridges, and people were actively trying *not* to communicate with him. Determined to reenter the world as a better version of himself, Jake had to figure out how to effectively interact with others in business and in life. Through this process, along with some deep study in human verbal and nonverbal communication, Jake became a master in the craft. He ultimately arrived at a point where he has now trained thousands of individuals and companies in his method of communication. And now, those hard-won ideas are in your hands.

As you're holding this book, you have three choices. You can set it aside and miss the opportunity. You can skim and gain a little. Or you can dig in, do the exercises, and transform the way you communicate. Whether at work, in sales, or at home, this book can transform how you interact in ways that benefit both you and those around you. I hope you decide to follow the third option like I have, so you too can communicate in an impactful way that adds meaning to the connections you have with others. Everyone in your life: your boss, clients, colleagues, family, and you yourself, will benefit if you adopt the methods in this book.

# TO THE READER

I didn't write this book from the top of the mountain. I wrote it because I know what it feels like to be at the bottom. Years ago, I lost my marriage, my home, and nearly everything else to addiction. In those moments, I wasn't just invisible, I was written off. People didn't take me seriously, and to be honest, I didn't take myself seriously either.

What I discovered on the climb back is that reinvention doesn't happen because you tell people you've changed. It happens when you change the way they see you. That's the heart of this book.

STRATA was born from that realization. It's not a bag of persuasion tricks. It's a system for awareness; learning to read others, notice the signals they send, and show up in a way that makes people feel seen and understood. Because when people feel understood, they open the door. And when the door opens, communication flows, trust builds, and action happens almost naturally.

Whether you're in a boardroom, a sales call, or sitting across the dinner table, the same truth applies: presence beats performance when performance can't get noticed. This book is about giving you the tools to make sure you are noticed, respected, and remembered.

My hope is simple: that by the time you finish these pages, you'll never walk into a room the same way again.

If at any time while reading this book, you feel you'd like to connect with one of my programs, turn back to this page and go to the website below.

www.thejakestahl.com

—Jake Stahl

# CONTENTS

# AUTHOR'S NOTE

If you're holding this book, it's probably not because you're bored. It's because there's a gap between what you know you're capable of and what people actually *see* in you. Maybe you've got the resume, the pitch deck, the talking points. Maybe you've been through leadership trainings, sales seminars, therapy. But there's still this moment—right before the meeting starts, before the conversation turns, before the deal closes—where things seem to slip.

That moment is what this book is about. That moment is what this book was built for.

This book is for the founder sitting across from investors who nod politely but never call back; for the sales leader with a burned-out team tired of roleplaying fake enthusiasm; for the account manager trying to win back a disengaged client; for the person in customer service who wants to stop reacting and start really understanding. But it's also for the people who feel misunderstood, like I once did. People who've been misread or mislabeled so many times they start to question if they'll ever be seen clearly again.

I wrote this book for you because I've been all of you.

There was a time in my life, not long ago, when I lost everything. My marriage. My house. My savings. My identity. Addiction wrecked it all. And at my lowest, I wasn't just dismissed, I was erased. People stopped calling. Doors closed. I became someone people avoided; someone they warned others about.

And I wouldn't take that time back for anything. That collapse forced me to strip away every performance, every role I thought I had to play. It made me ask questions most people avoid: Who am I when no one's watching? Who am I when no one *believes* in me? And who do I become if I stop trying to fix how I *look* and start changing how I *see*?

That reinvention didn't just shift how I saw myself. It transformed how I saw *others*. My recovery taught me that most people aren't responding to our words, they're responding to our presence; to how we show up; to what we trigger in them. It taught me to stop listening just for content and start listening for conflict, for patterns, for posture. I started watching people, not to judge, but to *understand*.

That's what the perception framework I call STRATA was born from. Not a whiteboard, not a marketing brainstorm, but from desperation. From real-world failure. From sitting across from people I loved, realizing I had no idea how to reach them. From learning the hard way that nobody changes until they feel *seen*.

This book is my attempt to make sure nobody else has to wait as long as I did to break free from being stuck. My "stuck" came from opioid addiction, but people become stuck for many reasons—alcohol, eating challenges, abuse, break-up, or even just a lack of motivation or a cycle of procrastination. Whatever it is that is holding you back, you can succeed in reaching your goals.

I want to give you permission—the kind I never had. Permission to try again. Permission to read people differently. Permission to approach your spouse, your boss, your clients, your kids with new eyes. Permission to see yourself not as someone behind or broken, but someone *becoming*.

Because it's not too late.

I'm 59 years old, and I've asked myself a hundred times if I've missed my window. If I'm too old to launch something new, too late to change how I do things. And I've decided that thought is a lie. If anything, I'm more equipped now than I ever was, because I've lived enough to know that the best strategies aren't the ones that sound smart. They're the ones that *work*. Under pressure. In real conversations. In messy boardrooms and even messier living rooms.

So yes, I want to challenge you but not with some empty, motivational rah-rah. I challenge you to *see people differently.* To stop reacting to the version of them you've rehearsed in your head and instead learn to read the actual version sitting in front of you. I challenge you to stop relying on scripts and start learning to track the signal, shift the energy, and build the kind of permission that makes everything else possible.

I wish someone had told me that 90% of communication isn't about what you *say*—it's about how you *show up.*

I wish someone had helped me understand that people are constantly adjusting their words based on how they read *you.* That posture is often more honest than language. That silence isn't always resistance, it's calculation. And that if you want to have more powerful conversations, you have to get fluent in the part of communication that happens *before* the first word is spoken.

Had I known this at the beginning of my career—not just as a trainer, but as a father, a husband, a human being—I would have saved myself a lot of heartache. I would have connected more deeply, sold more effectively, and led with more clarity. And maybe, just maybe, I wouldn't have needed to break down to finally understand it.

So here it is. No breakdown required.

This book isn't here to impress you. It's here to *equip* you. To give you a new way of listening. A new way of seeing. A new way of leading people toward action, not because you talk better, but because you *read others better.*

And if that sounds simple, it is. Using the STRATA framework isn't hard. But it is honest, and it works.

Thanks for walking this road with me. The first step has begun.

Let's change how you show up, affecting how you are seen by others.

Jake Stahl

# PREFACE

# THE LENS I HAD TO BUILD

*"We tell ourselves stories in order to live."*

— Joan Didion

*The pill bottle didn't make a loud sound when it tipped.*

*Just a soft click as it hit the counter.*

*No explosion. No fireworks.*

*But that was the moment I lost everything—my wife, my house, my name.*

*And the moment I started studying people like my life depended on it.*

*Because it did.*

## The Lens I Had to Build

STRATA is a perception framework that helps you read people, adjust your posture, and communicate effectively as if you're reading people's minds. I didn't create STRATA because I wanted to become a better communicator. I created it because I had to rebuild who I was from the inside out.

Twelve years ago, I was addicted to opioids. What started as pain relief became survival. And then it became hell. I lost my marriage. I lost my house. I drained my savings. And worse than all of that, I lost credibility to the world, to the people I loved, and to myself.

People didn't see me anymore. They saw a liability, a disappointment, a story they'd already decided the ending to. And every time I tried to prove I'd changed, I came off needy or fake or too polished. Because the harder you push for someone to see the *new you*, the more they double down on who they think you are.

So I stopped trying to explain myself. And I started studying what people were actually responding to.

Not their words—their *signals*.

Not their arguments—their *fears*.

Not their feedback—their *frame*.

I started noticing things in conversations I'd never noticed before. Body shifts. Pauses. Tells. Tension. I wasn't listening for agreement. I was listening for the moment *their guard dropped*. I wasn't selling. I was adjusting. Calibrating. Reading what was underneath. And then saying the one thing they didn't expect but needed to hear.

That was the beginning of STRATA. It didn't come from a marketing book or a sales training course. It came from survival. It came from losing everything. It came from needing a way back into rooms where I was already written off.

But over the next decade, the STRATA framework became something more. It helped me win deals no one thought were closable. It helped me raise kids who tell me things no one else gets to hear. It helped me understand the woman I love in ways I never knew how to before.

And now STRATA can be yours.

If you've ever walked away from a conversation thinking, *"Why didn't that land?"* ... If you've ever pitched your heart out and watched someone say "I'll think about it" while mentally walking away... If you've ever said the *right* thing and still lost the deal, the relationship, the room—this book is for you.

STRATA is the system I built when I couldn't afford to be misunderstood anymore. It's how I started seeing people clearly again. And how I got them to see me clearly in return. This isn't about persuasion. This isn't about pressure. It's about *precision*.

This book will teach you how to read people in real time. How to spot the exact moment influence gets blocked and how to unblock it. How to shift a conversation without pushing or posturing. And how to lead, sell, parent, coach, or love from a place of truth without losing your power.

You'll learn to hear what's not being said, to adjust before it's too late, to stop trying to be impressive, and to start being *in tune*.

That's the promise.

This is a book for people who are tired of being ignored. Tired of losing traction. Tired of talking to the "polished version" of someone and never reaching the real decision-maker behind their eyes.

If you've ever thought, *"I know I'm better than this moment is letting me be,"* welcome. You're exactly where you need to be.

Let's begin.

# CHAPTER 1

# YOU WERE NEVER IN THE ROOM

*"The single biggest problem in communication is the illusion that it has taken place."*

— George Bernard Shaw

*He didn't roll his eyes.*

*He didn't sigh.*

*He just leaned back slightly, checked his watch, and smiled like he already knew how this would end.*

*You hadn't said a word yet and somehow, you were already out of the room.*

## You Were Never in the Room

You felt it, didn't you? That flicker. That shift. The moment their face changed. You were saying all the right things, but something in their body said otherwise—tight jaw, folded arms, eyes that checked out while their mouth stayed polite.

And in that instant, the game was over. But you kept talking. You pitched harder. Explained more. Tried to reframe, to recover. You thought if you just clarified your point, or injected some charm, or *proved* your value a little better, you could win them back.

You couldn't. You were already gone.

Most people never realize when they've been dismissed. Not officially. No one says it out loud. But the decision's been made, and it wasn't about your logic, your slides, or your price. It was about your **presence**.

That's the part no one talks about.

We've been trained to believe communication is a game of words— articulate the message, deliver the value, make the case. But real influence doesn't happen at the level of information. It happens *before* that at the level of perception, emotion, and micro-behavior.

In other words: **how you show up speaks louder than anything you say.**

Let me be blunt. You've been taught to communicate in a world that doesn't exist anymore. You've been taught that clarity is king, that persuasion is about preparation, and that if you're good enough at explaining your worth, people will listen.

They won't.

Because you're not speaking to their logic. You're speaking to their fear. Their ego. Their urgency. You're speaking to someone who has already made up their mind by the time you open your mouth.

If you don't know how to read that—and adjust—then you were never in the conversation to begin with. But there is a solution.

Welcome to STRATA.

STRATA isn't a communication method. It's a **perception framework**. One that helps you read people in real time, adjust your posture, and identify the thing they're not saying out loud—but are begging someone to hear.

STRATA is built for the moments where logic fails. Where influence feels like it's slipping through your fingers. Where you walk away saying, "I thought it went well... so why didn't they move?"

STRATA is for sales calls. For job interviews. For boardrooms and bedrooms, and back-channel deals. But more than that, it's for the everyday conversations where your fate is being decided without you realizing it.

Let's get something clear: People don't buy your pitch. They buy your presence. They don't follow because you're smart. They follow because you *feel* right.

You can be right and still lose. Or you can be aligned and win before the facts are even discussed.

I learned this the hard way.

I remember this guy. Let's call him Eric.

A sales leader and polished as hell, Eric knew his product, had the stats, the case studies, the killer deck. He was pitching to a hospital system. A multi-million-dollar deal on the line. He called me in to coach him through the close because the meeting kept getting delayed. Stakeholders weren't responding. Something felt off.

So I sat in the back of the boardroom during the next meeting, just observing. Eric started strong, confident, structured. He walked through the pain points, anticipated objections, framed the value perfectly. Everything looked right on paper.

But I watched the medical director lean back, cross his arms, and glance at the CFO. The CFO didn't say a word, just tapped his pen. Quiet, subtle, but enough to shift the temperature of the room.

Eric didn't notice. He was too focused on finishing his deck. Too focused on delivering the "perfect pitch." They nodded, smiled, even said, "Thanks for coming in, this was helpful."

We walked out. Eric thought it went well. I looked him in the eye and said, "You lost the deal three minutes in."

He laughed. "No way. Did you see their faces? They were listening."

"No," I said. "They were deciding how to let you down gently."

And I'll never forget the moment that hit him. That flash of recognition. That sick feeling in his gut. Because it wasn't just *this* deal. It was a pattern. The dates that ghosted him. The clients who said "we'll circle back." The leadership teams that "wanted to think about it."

He wasn't failing because of his pitch. He was failing because he didn't know how to **read the shift.** He didn't clock the change in posture. Didn't pivot when the energy changed. Didn't adjust to the real room. He kept performing for the version he *wanted* to be there.

We dug into it and turned the meeting footage into a behavioral autopsy. And what we found wasn't just strategy, it was psychology.

He had been talking to the polished personas, the ones who nod, smile, perform their roles. But the decision was being made by the **hidden profile** in the room—the cautious one, the skeptical one, the ego-driven one. The version they don't show on LinkedIn, but the one who calls the shots.

Once Eric learned to see it, everything changed. He didn't get louder. He got quieter. He didn't double down. He redirected. And for the first time, the room leaned *in* instead of pulling away.

The problem is, we think we're being clear. We think our message is landing. We mistake politeness for engagement. We confuse nodding with buying. But underneath the surface, there's always another layer. A signal. A trigger. A belief. A posture. A reflex. A need.

Most people don't know how to see that, let alone respond to it. STRATA gives you the lens to read the room before it reads you. It's not about manipulation. It's about matching the **moment**, so your message has a place to land.

4

Because communication isn't about saying the right thing. It's about saying the right thing **in the right way** to the **right version** of the person in front of you.

Most people are pitching to a lie. They're speaking to the polished version, the mask, the role, the professional persona.

STRATA shows you how to speak to the real one. The one who makes the decisions. The one who carries the fear. The one who needs what you offer but can't admit it yet.

While trying to make a deal, you're not here to be impressive. You're here to be read. And once you're read, then you get to read them back. That's when the conversation really starts.

STRATA stands for:

> **Signal** – What you broadcast before you speak.
>
> **Trigger** – The moment resistance surfaces.
>
> **Reframe** – How you pivot their perception.
>
> **Anchor** – How you cement the shift.
>
> **Transfer** – The moment influence becomes theirs.
>
> **Action** – What moves them, finally, to say yes.

Each chapter ahead will walk you through one of these layers.

You'll learn to spot what others miss. To feel the moment when a buyer pulls away, or leans in. To say the thing they're not saying out loud, but desperately need someone to name. And to move people, not by force, but by frictionless alignment.

We'll go deep, but never abstract. This book is built to be used. The examples are real. The stories are raw. And the frameworks are teachable.

Let's get started.

# CHAPTER 2

# THE MESSAGE BENEATH THE MESSAGE

*"What you do speaks so loudly that I cannot hear what you say."*

— Ralph Waldo Emerson

*She nodded at your deck.*

*Smiled at your points.*

*Laughed politely at your story.*

*And then said, "Let me think about it."*

*But her foot had already turned toward the door fifteen minutes ago.*

*The yes was in her voice.*

*The no was in her body.*

## The Message Beneath the Message

Before a word is spoken, the conversation has already begun. You walk into a room, shake a hand, open a Zoom window, or even send a cold email and without realizing it, you've already said more than most people say in an hour.

Because signal isn't what you say. Signal is what they see. It's your body. Your timing. Your tone. Your urgency. Your silence. Your breath. Your rhythm. Your presence. And it's being read whether you mean for it to or not.

If Chapter 1 was the awakening, realizing that most conversations are lost before they begin, then this chapter is your first tool in flipping that script. Signal is the first layer of STRATA for a reason. Nothing else matters if the first impression collapses.

Let me tell you a story.

A woman, let's call her Amanda, was leading a product demo. Sharp, well-rehearsed, and incredibly smart, Amanda had built the product herself, and she knew it better than anyone. But the moment a client joined the call, Amanda shifted. She sat up straighter, her voice went up a pitch, and she started speaking faster, smiling more, and trying to sound "friendly."

These actions weren't conscious. They were instinct. But here's what the client saw: someone uncertain. Someone selling. Someone compensating. The client didn't read her words. They read her signal.

And that's the paradox. Amanda was confident. She did know the material, but the signal she sent—the one below the surface—told a different story. And that's what the client bought. Or in her case, didn't buy. We fixed it, of course. But not by changing the script. We changed the signal.

Signal is about congruence—the alignment between what you're saying and how you're showing up while saying it. When those things match, you gain trust even if your message isn't perfect. But when they don't, even the most polished pitch starts to feel off. Inauthentic. Pushed. Signal is the vibe before the voice. It's the undercurrent of the entire interaction.

And the wild thing is... it's not just that people are picking up your signal. It's that they're doing it without realizing it. We're wired for it. Mirror neurons. Somatic markers. Evolutionary reflexes. The brain doesn't wait for logic; it scans for threat, warmth, status, permission. So when someone says, "I don't know, something just felt off..." what they're reacting to is your signal.

If you want to be taken seriously in the first five seconds, you need to know exactly what signal you're sending—and why.

Here's what most people get wrong. They try to fake confidence by mimicking posture. They try to fake urgency by speeding up. They try to fake authority by lowering their voice. But signal isn't a trick. It's a read. And your audience is better at detecting inconsistency than you are at performing.

Because signal isn't just a projection; it's a conversation. It doesn't live in your body. It lives in the space between you and the other person. It's dynamic. It changes. It echoes. And it either opens a door or closes it.

In STRATA, we break signal down into five distinct lenses:

- Posture
- Urgency
- Tone
- Rhythm
- Presence

Each one tells a story before your words ever get the chance.

## Posture: The Physical Story You're Telling

Posture is the first thing they notice and often the last thing they trust. Not your shoulders. Not your spine. Not just how you stand. I'm talking about your psychological posture. The story your body tells about your status, your comfort, your readiness.

When someone has good posture, we say they look "grounded." Like they belong. When someone has bad posture, we say they look "off." Like they're trying too hard. This isn't about standing tall like your mom told you. It's about alignment. Does your body reflect the outcome you expect?

Because that's the test. If you expect to be ignored, your body folds. If you expect to be challenged, your body braces. If you expect to be accepted, your body relaxes and holds space.

I once coached a founder who always crossed his arms during pitches. Not because he was closed off but because he was uncomfortable being seen. He wanted the deal, but his signal said, "Don't look too closely."

So I asked him, "What would your body look like if you assumed they already said yes?" He paused. Sat back. Uncrossed his arms. Spoke slower. Held eye contact. That was the real version of him, the one who closes deals. The posture didn't just shift his body. It shifted his signal.

Posture is your first invitation or your first warning. And it always shows up before your pitch does.

So, how do you change your posture?

Before you even speak, your posture is already telling the room what to expect. The trick isn't to fake confidence—it's to anchor yourself before you cross the threshold. Pause at the door. Plant your feet. Breathe once, slowly. Let your shoulders settle back instead of rising up. And then walk in like the deal is already done. Not cocky, not casual—just assured. That small reset shifts you from "hoping to be accepted" into "ready to be heard." People notice. They may not know why, but they feel it.

## Urgency: The Pressure You Broadcast Without Meaning To

Urgency isn't about speed. It's about tension. When someone speaks quickly because they're excited, we feel their energy. But when they speak quickly because they're afraid you'll walk away, we feel their anxiety. The same action. Two totally different signals.

Urgency shows up in your pace, yes. But also your breathing, your phrasing, your pauses, or lack of them. It's your way of telling the room: this matters... or this might slip away.

But here's the kicker: when you're urgent for the wrong reason, your posture collapses. You rush. You crowd. You over-explain. You force a close that hasn't been earned. You stop leading and start chasing.

I worked with a rep once who sold beautifully when she didn't care about the deal. Calm. Clear. Crisp. But the moment the deal was high-stakes, or the client was someone she wanted to impress, her urgency spiked. Her voice sped up. She repeated herself. Her hands fidgeted.

She wasn't excited. She was afraid of losing. And that fear leaked out of every word. The client didn't need to analyze it. They just felt it. Something felt tight. Something felt off. So they pulled away.

Urgency isn't about removing pressure, it's about directing it. When your urgency comes from clarity, confidence, and the knowledge that what you're saying deserves to land, it hits differently. You don't have to rush. You don't have to force. You just hold the space and make them come forward.

The fastest way to shift your urgency is to flip your attention. Instead of thinking, *Do they like me? Will they say yes?* Anchor to *Does this matter? Do I believe it belongs here?* When urgency comes from belief instead of fear, your pace slows down naturally. Breathe at the end of your sentences. Let silence work for you. Hold eye contact without rushing to fill it. That's how you keep the pressure in the room but on the right side of the table.

Urgency is one of the most misread signals in business. Because it wears a mask of enthusiasm... while hiding a heart of desperation. When you can recognize the difference in yourself, and others, you stop reacting to surface behavior, and you start reading what's real.

## Tone: What They Feel—Even If You Never Meant It

Tone is the emotional fingerprint of your signal. It's the reason the same sentence can land as a joke, a threat, a plea, or a command depending on how you say it. You could say, "I need to talk to you," and have it sound urgent, intimate, controlling, curious, or completely unbothered. The words are fixed. The tone is not.

And that's where most people lose their audience, because they're focused on scripting language instead of controlling emotional resonance. People don't remember your words. They remember how your words felt.

Tone is where your beliefs leak out. You may say, "I'm confident in this plan," but if your tone says, "I'm nervous you'll push back," then that's the version that gets heard. And once that version is heard, good luck trying to convince them otherwise.

Tone is incredibly revealing. If you carry resentment, it will sneak into your tone as sharpness or condescension. If you're trying to please, it will show up as hesitation or over-eagerness. If you feel beneath them, your tone will defer. If you feel above them, your tone will challenge. Even if your words are perfect.

I once worked with an executive who couldn't figure out why her team wasn't responding to her strategy sessions. She was brilliant, thoughtful, and her plans made sense on paper. But I sat in on a few of her meetings and caught the mismatch.

Her tone was flat. Not calm. Not confident. Just... flat. Detached. Slightly defensive. She sounded like she was trying to prove something without showing it. Her team didn't feel inspired, they felt like they were being talked at.

The fix wasn't in the content. It was in the tone of conviction. We did vocal drills. We rewired how she started each session. We grounded her in the why behind her message. And her tone shifted from "read this slide" to "rally this mission." And guess what? The team leaned in. Because they could finally feel her in the room.

Tone matters because it's how people decide whether to trust what they see. It doesn't just support your signal. It is your signal. And if your tone is off, nothing else can land. The solution is as easy as being intentional about your tone.

## Rhythm: The Invisible Tempo of Connection

Rhythm is what makes a message feel alive, or robotic. It's not just how fast or slow you talk. It's the timing between your ideas, your pauses, your inflections. It's the sync between your delivery and the listener's breath.

Rhythm is what keeps people with you or leaves them behind.

Ever listened to someone whose pace felt just right? Who paused in the places that made you lean in? Who knew when to let a sentence land without rushing to the next one? That's rhythm. And it's not an accident.

The best communicators understand how to pace a room. They don't just deliver information, they score it like music. They know when to slow down for emphasis, when to pick up for energy, when to pause so the point can hit.

But most people don't think about rhythm. They think about content. So their signal feels mechanical. Flat. Predictable. Or worse... overwhelming.

I once coached a young sales director. He was brilliant, articulate, and sharp as hell. But his rhythm was relentless. Like he was sprinting through the pitch. He spoke in bursts. No breath. No space. No silence.

He thought it sounded dynamic. To the client, it felt like pressure.

To highlight this, I recorded him and played it back. And when he listened, he actually said, "I sound like I'm nervous they'll hang up." Exactly. That was the signal.

We worked on cadence. Pacing. Letting ideas breathe. Within two weeks, he was closing more deals, not because his message changed, but because the rhythm of his message finally gave people space to trust it.

Rhythm isn't about slowing down. It's about matching the moment. Sometimes rhythm means speed and intensity. Sometimes rhythm means stillness and silence. But it always means timing. And if your rhythm is off, your signal gets scrambled even if every other piece is right.

## Presence: The Real You That Shows Up—or Doesn't

Presence is the single most important part of your signal. Because presence is the feeling people get when they sense you're fully here. Not distracted. Not performative. Not rehearsing your next line or silently negotiating with your nerves. Here. Grounded. Unshakable.

And here's the magic of presence: when it's real, everything else clicks. Your posture settles. Your urgency relaxes. Your tone deepens. Your rhythm flows. Presence doesn't mean stillness. It doesn't mean dominance. It means full availability. To the moment. To the room. To the truth of what's happening right now.

When you're present, people feel safer because they know you're actually with them. When you're not, people don't always know why they feel off. They just sense it. You're disconnected. Performing. Somewhere else.

I worked with a VP once who had all the skills. Every box checked. But his team never brought him bad news. They never spoke up early when projects veered off track. He asked me why. I said, "Because when you're in the room, you're not really in the room."

He was constantly scanning for what to say next. Trying to manage the meeting instead of participate in it. We trained his nervous system to settle. To breathe into eye contact. To listen instead of waiting to speak. And suddenly, people opened up.

Presence doesn't happen by accident. It's a discipline. A practice of being undistracted. Of owning your space without filling it with noise.

If signal is how people decide whether to trust you, presence is what convinces them you're worth hearing out.

## Signal Recap: What You Send Before You Speak

Let's bring it all together:

- Posture sets the physical tone: do you belong here, or are you bracing for rejection?
- Urgency reveals your internal pressure: are you leading the pace or chasing approval?
- Tone exposes emotional subtext: are your words aligned with what you really believe?
- Rhythm governs your delivery: does your pace let the message land, or overwhelm it?
- Presence glues it all together: are you fully here, or just playing a part?

These five lenses make up your signal. They're already being read. The only question is whether you're sending them on purpose. Because when your signal lands right, you don't have to convince anyone. You don't have to push. You don't have to perform.

You simply show up clear, grounded, congruent and the room calibrates to you. That's the power of signal. And once you can read it in yourself, you can start reading it in them.

Which brings us to the second layer of STRATA: Trigger.

Because the moment someone's signal shifts... that's when the real conversation begins. That's where resistance hides. That's where opportunity lives. And that's what we'll uncover in Chapter 3.

# CHAPTER 3

# TRIGGER – THE MOMENT RESISTANCE SPEAKS

*"Every action has a reason. The trick is knowing where the fire started—not just where the smoke is."*

— Unknown

*You mentioned a pricing change, and his face didn't move.*

*Not one twitch. Not one blink.*

*But his pen stopped. Mid-sentence.*

*And that's when the conversation left the rails.*

*Not because of the number.*

*But because you touched the scar and didn't know it.*

## Trigger – The Moment Resistance Speaks

You don't lose the deal at the close. You lose it at the flinch.

Not the big dramatic kind; the subtle one. A slight shift in posture. A delay in response. A word they repeat back to you with just a little edge.

That's the trigger. It's not resistance yet. Not outright objection. But it's the first sign something underneath is stirring. The question is: Do you catch it? Most people don't. They keep going. Pushing forward. Following their agenda while the other person's brain has already stepped sideways. You thought you were still in the conversation. But they've already started protecting themselves.

Trigger is the second layer of STRATA because it's the moment when perception collides with belief. Your presence bumps into their wiring. Your signal hits their filter. Your confidence meets their story, and that story pushes back.

You've seen it a thousand times. You're in flow, and then the energy shifts. Their face goes still. Their voice drops. Their answers get clipped, or overly polite. They say "Interesting…" but mean "No." They say "I'll think about it…" but mean "I'm already gone."

What changed? You hit a trigger. And unless you know how to spot it, and address it, it will run the rest of the conversation without you.

Most people miss triggers because they're trained to look for logic. They expect objections to be rational. Vocal. Formal. But triggers live in the nervous system. They're primal. Fast. Somatic. Subconscious. Someone hears a certain word and tenses. Someone sees a certain price and freezes. Feels a certain tone and gets defensive, without knowing why.

And if you're not trained to catch that moment, you'll spend the rest of the conversation talking to someone who's no longer open.

However, the trigger doesn't have to be a problem. It can be a portal. It tells you where the story is stuck. It shows you where the belief lives. And if you respond to it with awareness, not pressure, you earn trust faster than any pitch ever could.

When you can name the moment they flinch, you don't lose them. You lead them. And that's where the real influence begins.

But before we go further, let's draw a clear line. Signal and Trigger are not the same.

Signal is what *you send*—the energy, posture, and presence you broadcast into the room in a certain moment.

Trigger is what *you activate* in them.

It's a ripple effect. The emotional bruise you brushed up against. The subconscious alarm system that flares when something you said, or the way you said it, touched a belief they didn't know was still raw.

So when a client clenches their jaw or freezes for a beat, that's not the trigger, it's the **signal of the trigger**. The jaw clench is the flare. The trigger is what caused it.

Maybe it was fear of risk. Maybe it was resentment toward a past vendor. Maybe it was shame around not understanding something technical. Whatever it is, it lives below the surface. And you don't get to see it directly—you only get the moment it shows up in the body.

That's why this layer of STRATA isn't just about watching. It's about translating.

Which brings me a guy we'll call Adam.

Adam was a top rep at a tech firm I consulted for. He was well-liked, articulate, full of drive. His numbers were strong, but he kept plateauing with the enterprise deals. His managers chalked it up to bad timing, tough committees, or pricing pressure. But I knew better. Adam didn't have a strategy problem. He had a trigger blindness problem.

I watched one of his calls with a major buyer. At first, it was smooth. He was aligned, warm, confident. But then, as he laid out the platform's long-term roadmap, the client did something small; so small Adam didn't notice. The man's jaw tightened. Just slightly. His eyes narrowed. His pen stopped moving.

Adam didn't see it. He kept going. Five more minutes of features, integrations, cost-saving logic. And the deal never moved forward.

When I showed Adam the clip, I paused it at that exact second. "That's it," I said. "Right there. That's the shift."

"That?" he asked. "He just looked down."

"Exactly. He looked down because you hit something he didn't want to deal with yet. Probably long-term integration anxiety. Or regret from a past rollout that went sideways. You didn't lose him at the end, you lost him the second you ignored that moment."

That's the power of trigger. It's not loud. It's not formal. But it's final if you miss it.

Triggers show up in facial expressions, vocal stress, breathing, fidgeting, deflection. And they often happen in response to very specific things: pricing language, status comparisons, abstract future framing, loss of control, emotional vulnerability, time pressure.

Triggers are not random. They're patterned. And once you learn to read the patterns, you can shift your language, your posture, your energy right when it counts.

We'll go deeper into how to read these in the next section, but for now, I want you to understand this: triggers are not a failure of your pitch. They are the **beginning** of trust. When someone flinches, they're telling you what matters. They're showing you where they've been burned. Where they carry doubt. Where their internal model is trying to protect them from risk.

You don't fight that. You don't bulldoze through it. You **honor it** and redirect it.

That's what we'll do next.

So how do you actually read a trigger in real time?

You begin by slowing down, not just your speech or your movement, but your awareness. It's a perceptual shift. Most people are moving so quickly through their script, their pitch, or even their day, that they miss the moment when the energy in the room changes. A shift in eye contact, the way someone starts repeating your language instead of generating their own, a subtle shift in posture or breath—these are not random. They are the body's early warning system, firing before the mind has caught up. You didn't lose their interest. You bumped into something inside them that wasn't ready.

Reading triggers requires discipline. It's not a dramatic intuition or psychic skill, it's pattern recognition. And like any pattern, once you know what to look for, you can't unsee it. A sudden stillness. The delay between your question and their answer. The flicker of doubt when price is mentioned. The tightening jaw when you bring up a past implementation.

But more than noticing, it's how you respond that sets you apart. When most people sense tension, they try to push through it. They speed up. They try to explain. They try to win. But the real strategy is to zoom in. Hold space. Stay grounded. And name the shift.

That might sound something like, "That landed differently. Want to walk through it?" Or, "I saw something shift just now. Let's pause there." You're not calling them out. You're inviting them forward. You're telling them, with your tone and timing, that tension doesn't scare you and that you're not here to overpower them, you're here to read them.

This is where trust is built. In the micro-moments. In the calm curiosity. In the choice not to skip the signal.

Before we get into the five most common types of psychological triggers, and how to respond to each, I want you to sit with this: people flinch when something matters. The reaction isn't the problem. It's the roadmap.

If you learn how to read that roadmap, you stop dancing around objections, and start dissolving them before they even fully form.

That's where we're headed next.

There are five core types of psychological triggers you'll see most often in the field. Each one is rooted in a different emotional reflex. Understanding these doesn't just make you better at handling objections. It makes you better at reading people.

The first is the **Control Trigger.**

This is activated when someone feels their autonomy is being threatened. It shows up in buyers who suddenly say, "Let me think about it," right after you ask a closing question, or who start asserting unrelated authority like, "Well, I've been doing this for 25 years." What they're reacting to isn't your offer. It's the feeling of being cornered. The way out isn't to push harder, it's to hand control back. You shift from pressure to permission. "I'll lay out the options. You decide how we move forward." It's subtle, but it reopens the door.

Second is the **Competence Trigger.**

This happens when someone feels exposed, confused, or like they might look stupid. It often shows up in technical demos, financial breakdowns, or discussions of long-term implementation. The signal here might be a quiet withdrawal, a repeated nod, or an overuse of phrases like "Yeah, yeah, I got it." Don't mistake that for buy-in. They're signaling shame. Your move shouldn't be to dumb it down, it's to slow the frame and validate the complexity. "This part tends to be where questions come up. Want to walk through it together?" That one sentence preserves their competence without letting confusion calcify into resistance.

Third is the **Status Trigger.**

This one's tricky, because it can be either overt or deeply buried. You'll notice it when someone who seemed engaged suddenly becomes cold, dismissive, or even sarcastic. What you likely triggered is a subconscious threat to their position. Maybe they're not the real decision-maker, and they're trying to save face. Maybe you've outpaced them socially or intellectually without realizing it. To diffuse this, you don't minimize yourself, you elevate them. Ask for input. Highlight their leadership. Let them reestablish footing.

Fourth is the **Value Trigger**.

This shows up when someone feels that what you're offering doesn't align with what they care about most. It often surfaces as lukewarm agreement: "Yeah, makes sense," followed by silence. The problem isn't your pitch, it's the lens. You're solving a problem they don't feel yet. Or you're solving it in a language they don't connect with. The fix here is simple: stop describing the feature. Start describing the pain. "Tell me what's felt most expensive about doing nothing up to this point." That flips the conversation from product to priority.

The last is the **Time Trigger**.

This one's everywhere. The energy drops. The urgency disappears. "Maybe next quarter." "We're just not ready." But time is rarely about time. It's almost always code for fear. Fear of change. Fear of commitment. Fear of taking the next step and it not working. The move here isn't to create false urgency. It's to isolate the fear under the delay. "Let's say it's next quarter. What would need to be different between now and then to make it a yes?" That moves the conversation from someday to strategy.

These five triggers aren't the only ones you'll see, but they're the most common. And once you know how to spot them, you'll realize most objections aren't really about money, time, or fit. They're about identity. Safety. Clarity. Power. When you learn to address those softly, directly, with presence, you stop convincing. You start unlocking.

And that's what this entire chapter has been about: recognizing that the moment someone resists you isn't the end of the conversation. It's the beginning of the real one. When you understand triggers, you stop reacting to symptoms and start addressing root causes. You see the hesitation, not as a rejection, but as a reflection of a deeper need. You adjust, not to manipulate, but to meet them where they are, not where you wish they were.

You'll walk into fewer conversations thinking you need to be impressive, and more conversations focused on being aware. You'll notice the jaw clench, the glance away, the too-easy agreement and instead of missing your window, you'll use it. You'll pivot. You'll re-engage. And most of all, you'll do it without losing your presence.

People don't want to be convinced. They want to be seen. And when you meet the trigger with calm precision, you become someone worth trusting.

Which brings us to the next layer of STRATA: **Reframe**.

You've read the signal. You've identified the trigger. But now you have to *move the moment* to shift the way they see the situation, the offer, or even themselves.

Reframe is where tension becomes transformation.

And that's what we'll explore in Chapter 4.

# CHAPTER 4

# REFRAME – THE SHIFT THAT CHANGES EVERYTHING

*"We don't see things as they are, we see them as we are."*

— Anaïs Nin

*She was dead set against it.*

*You could've had the Pope co-sign and she'd still say no.*

*Until you said,*

*"I'm not asking you to change your mind—I'm asking you to look at it through their eyes."*

*And suddenly, she wasn't fighting you anymore.*

*She was defending her own new idea.*

## Reframe – The Shift That Changes Everything

Every conversation is a negotiation between worldviews. Not just about price, or value, or decision-making authority. But about what's safe, what's true, and what's possible. The person sitting across from you isn't just evaluating your offer., they're measuring it against their existing story.

And if your message doesn't fit their frame? It gets rejected, not because it's wrong, but because it's *foreign*. That's why you need to learn how to reframe. Because once you've read the signal and named the trigger, the next step is movement. Internal movement. A pivot in how they see the problem, the path, or even themselves.

Reframe is not about tricking someone. It's not a clever comeback. It's not spin. Reframe is the art of helping someone look at the same reality through a new lens and feel different enough to take action.

Think about it. Have you ever heard someone say, "I never thought about it like that before," and then suddenly they're open again? That's the power of a reframe. It dissolves resistance without a fight. It sidesteps ego. It introduces possibility into a space that was locked.

Most resistance isn't about the facts; it's about the frame. And if you keep arguing inside the old frame, you lose. Every time. But if you can gently, clearly, and confidently shift the lens… everything opens.

In this chapter, we'll show you how. But before we dive into the techniques, you need to understand what makes a reframe powerful.

It's not about sounding smart. It's not about winning an argument or spinning a better version of your offer. A real reframe meets the other person *inside* their current belief and then shifts what they *believe is possible*.

You can't reframe unless you know what frame you're working inside of. And that means listening, not just for facts, but for structure. Are they viewing this conversation through a lens of scarcity? Past failure? Powerlessness? Burnout? Competition? Fear of risk? Ego protection?

Whatever that lens is, it's shaping what they hear and what they block.

Let's take a simple example. A CFO hears the words "long-term value" and flinches. You could try to explain harder, but they're not in a frame that can process "value." They're in a frame of risk. Of cost. Of short-term exposure. So you reframe: "This isn't about committing to long-term value. It's about not bleeding short-term margin while waiting for a better option that isn't coming."

Same offer. New lens. And now, it lands. You didn't push them. You *pivoted them.*

The power of a reframe is in its precision and its **emotional logic.** It needs to feel true *enough* to bypass defensiveness and different *enough* to create movement. That means the best reframes don't sound like brilliant one-liners. They sound like truth the person almost already knew. They feel like a light switch flipped on.

Let me show you what this looks like in the real world.

A while back, I was coaching a founder. He was a sharp guy, mid-40s, running a tight SaaS business but he was burning out. He came to me thinking he needed help motivating his team. He said they weren't pushing hard enough. That they weren't hungry.

So we sat down, and I started asking questions. Within minutes, I could tell the real issue wasn't the team. It was him. He didn't trust them to lead. Every task had to go through him. Every decision was second-guessed. He thought he was being thorough, but he was suffocating the system.

When I gently pointed that out, he flinched. Got defensive. Started telling me how high the stakes were and how he couldn't afford mistakes. That was the trigger.

This is an old story: *If I let go, everything falls apart.* I could've tried to argue. Could've pointed to the inefficiency, the lost time, the stress. But none of that would've worked. Not inside that frame.

So I said: "Right now, your team's not underperforming. They're under-trusted. You think you're preventing failure but what you're actually doing is robbing them of ownership. You're holding it all together, but you're also holding it all back."

He didn't say anything; just sat there. Then he looked up and said, "Shit. That's exactly what my wife told me last week." That was the flip. The moment it clicked. The moment the frame shifted from *they're the problem* to *I'm holding the wheel too tightly.* And after that? Everything changed. He didn't just delegate more. He delegated with presence. With trust. And the team rose to meet it.

That's the power of a reframe. You don't force it. You *find* it. You listen for the belief underneath the behavior and then you pivot it, just enough for someone to see their own story differently.

Now, let's walk through the five most effective reframe types:

1. **Urgency Reframe** – From pressure to timing. When someone resists urgency, it's usually because they associate it with being cornered. They feel rushed, not prioritized. The urgency reframe isn't about turning up the volume, it's about shifting the *reason* for speed. For example: "I'm not trying to push you. I'm trying to protect your options. The longer we wait, the fewer you'll have." That reframe softens the pressure and recasts the timeline as an act of service.

2. **Ego Reframe** – From fear of looking weak to a moment of strength. This is especially powerful in leadership conversations. Someone resists a change because they're afraid it will signal incompetence. The reframe? "The people who shift fastest aren't the ones who were wrong, they're the ones who care enough to evolve." You're reframing adaptation as strength, not retreat.

3. **Risk Reframe** – From fear of loss to cost of delay. Most buyers don't fear *buying*; they fear *regret*. They're trying to avoid making a mistake that they'll pay for. Instead of pretending the risk isn't real, shift the focus: "You're not deciding whether or not to take a risk, you're deciding which risk is more acceptable: trying something imperfect now or waiting and falling further behind."

4. **Identity Reframe** – From fixed role to flexible power. Sometimes people resist because they're locked in an identity: the fixer, the skeptic, the provider, the protector. Reframing lets them see that identity in a new light. "You're not stepping back. You're stepping up into a version of leadership that doesn't require you to do it all yourself." You're not dismantling their identity. You're expanding it.

5. **Possibility Reframe** – From constraint to control. When someone says, "I don't have the time," or "We've never done it that way," they're locked in a frame of limitation. The reframe flips that: "Exactly. And that's why it's yours to change. Nobody's done it because they weren't in your position." You turn the block into a permission slip.

Each of these reframes works because it doesn't argue with the current belief. It *builds a bridge from it.* It respects where someone is and then gives them a compelling reason to move. The goal isn't to dominate the conversation. It's to reopen it. And once you master that skill, resistance stops feeling like a threat and starts becoming the map.

That's why Reframe is the hinge point of STRATA. Signal gets you noticed. Trigger tells you where the tension is. But Reframe? That's the turn. The moment the story opens. It's when you stop reacting to resistance and start rewriting the rules of engagement.

Reframe is not a tactic. It's a discipline. It's about staying present when most people panic. It's about reaching for understanding when others double down on explanation. And above all, it's about moving the conversation to higher ground where logic, emotion, and momentum can finally align.

Once you shift the story, something else happens too: you create space for a new identity to emerge. One that isn't bound by the old constraints. One that sees possibility where there used to be protection. And that's where we go next.

But before we leave this chapter, let's ground what we've learned in a few real-life examples—moments where a reframe changed not just the direction of a conversation, but the emotional outcome it created.

## The Executive Who Couldn't Say No

I once worked with a senior VP of sales who was chronically overcommitted. She said yes to every internal meeting, responded personally to every email, and tried to be available to everyone on her team. She thought she was being a servant leader. What she was actually doing was burning out.

When I asked her why she couldn't delegate or delay, she got quiet. Then she said, "Because if I'm not available, I'm not valuable." That was the frame.

I didn't try to counter it. I said, "So your value is tied to how reactive you are?"

She paused. "I guess... yeah."

And then I said: "What if the most valuable people aren't reactive? What if they're rare? Available when it counts, but unavailable by design because their time is already protecting higher-leverage work?"

That landed. Her shoulders dropped. She leaned back. And I could see it click. The reframe wasn't about productivity. It was about **permission** to stop measuring her worth by her willingness to self-sacrifice. That's the hidden power of a reframe: not just clarity, but **liberation**.

## The Deal Stuck in Fear of Change

A client was about to make a major tech transition. Everyone on the buying team saw the value except one holdout. A senior stakeholder who kept delaying the final approval.

When I finally got him on a call, I didn't push features or ROI. I asked what his biggest fear was. He said, "It's not that I don't believe this could work. It's that I've made a big change before… and it blew up in my face." He wasn't afraid of the product. He was afraid of the **echo**.

So I said: "It sounds like your experience isn't what's holding you back. It's what's making you qualified to get this right."

He looked at me and said, "Say that again."

I did. Slowly. And that's when he leaned forward. "Alright. Let's do this."

It wasn't logic that moved him. It was being **seen**, not as someone resisting, but someone protecting. That's the nuance reframes allow. They don't flatten resistance. They dignify it and then shift its shape.

## Reframing for Yourself

Here's something most people don't realize: reframes aren't just something you do for others. They're a skill you must turn inward.

Every time you say, "I'm not ready," or "I'm not like them," or "This always happens to me," you're living inside a frame, a belief that shapes your behavior. And if you never challenge it, it becomes your default lens.

I've had to reframe my own story a hundred times, especially when I was rebuilding my life from rock bottom. I could've stayed in the frame of shame. Of regret. Of 'proving I'm not who they thought I was.' But that story was never going to serve me. So I rewrote the frame: "They didn't see me because I hadn't learned how to show up yet. That's on me and it's also my edge now."

When you take ownership of your lens, you stop waiting for external validation. You stop seeking safety in sameness. And you start learning how to lead from your own evolution. This is what STRATA teaches you, chapter by chapter.

You're not just learning how to win the room. You're learning how to **change what the room is willing to believe.** And now that you can reframe with clarity and confidence, we move to the next frontier.

Let's anchor that belief and make it stick.

# CHAPTER 5

# ANCHOR – MAKING IT STICK

*"They may forget what you said—but they will never forget how you made them feel."*

— Maya Angelou

*He kept repeating the data.*

*Over and over.*

*"This is a smart decision," he said.*

*But his team kept hesitating.*

*Because smart doesn't close the loop.*

*Safe does.*

*Felt does.*

*That's where commitment lives.*

## Anchor – Making It Stick

There's a moment in every powerful interaction, right after the shift has happened, where the air changes. You've read the signal. You've named the trigger. You've reframed the resistance and watched their shoulders drop, their eyes flicker with new possibility. And in that instant, they're open.

But openness doesn't mean ownership.

Not yet. Because just as quickly as that window opens, it can slam shut again. The old story starts creeping back in. The doubts return. The environment pushes back. They forget. Or worse, they question whether they ever truly believed what you helped them see in the first place.

That's where **Anchor** comes in.

Anchor is the fourth layer of STRATA because it's the hinge between insight and integration. It's what prevents a breakthrough from becoming a blip. It's the difference between someone nodding in agreement and someone walking out of the room changed.

Let's be blunt: most conversations die on the vine not because they were weak... but because they were *unanchored*. The shift was real, but it was never sealed. Anchoring isn't about repetition. It's not about driving a point home until it sticks. It's about giving the new belief a place to live. A form. A weight. A memory. Something that keeps it rooted especially when the old patterns try to reclaim the ground.

Think about how this shows up in the real world. A sales leader runs a brilliant team call. Everyone's fired up. They've just realigned on vision, broken through a major bottleneck, committed to a fresh strategy. But two weeks later, behaviors haven't changed. Performance hasn't shifted. The same excuses are creeping back in.

Why? Because the message didn't stick. It was water through fingers energizing in the moment, gone by Monday.

Anchor turns that moment into a milestone. So how do you actually **anchor** a new belief or behavior?

There are three core principles:

1. **Emotion seals it.**

2. Ownership cements it.

3. Context protects it.

We'll unpack each one in depth. But first, let me show you what happens when anchoring is missing.

## The Unanchored Deal

I was brought in to consult on a high-stakes enterprise deal. It was seven figures, multiple stakeholders, months of relationship equity on the line. My client had done everything right. They'd built rapport, delivered the pitch, responded to every objection, and finally had the economic buyer nodding, ready to go.

Except he didn't.

The buyer said, "Let me think on it." And two weeks later, the whole thing unraveled. The buyer ghosted. The momentum died. The company went with a competitor.

When they came to me, shell-shocked, I asked to hear the pitch. I sat back, listened, and sure enough, there it was. Every signal read perfectly. The buyer's trigger was crystal clear: fear of past vendor failure. They'd reframed it beautifully, positioning their solution as the low-risk bet.

But then... silence. They never *sealed* it. Never anchored the new belief that "this time could be different." They assumed the logic was enough. It wasn't. You can't expect people to walk around holding your best insight in their head like a trophy. You have to make it live inside them. You have to *build the anchor*.

Let's start with the first principle.

## Emotion Seals It

All behavior is state-dependent.

35

That means people don't act based on what they *know*; they act based on what they *feel* in the moment a decision is made. And if you want your influence to last, the feeling that created it needs to be easy to *relive*. That's what an anchor does.

When a Navy SEAL learns to stay calm under gunfire, it's not because they have superior logic, it's because their emotional system has been conditioned to attach calm to chaos. That's an anchor.

When a performer hits the same mark on stage, night after night, with the same surge of intensity, it's because that mark *means* something. It's not just a location. It's a trigger for presence.

For your message to stick, it needs an **emotional fingerprint**.

This is why stories are so powerful. Metaphors. Imagery. Physical cues. They give your audience a *feeling*, not just a fact. And that feeling becomes the handle they can grab when the old behavior tries to take over.

Think about a time when someone said something that truly changed you. I'll bet you don't remember the entire conversation. But you remember the *moment*. The pause. The intensity. The internal *click*. That's the emotional anchor. Without it, the idea evaporates.

Let me give you a quick story. A woman I was coaching was terrified of public speaking. She kept saying, "I freeze. I can't breathe. I'm not like them." So we reframed it. We made it about service, not performance. About being a message carrier, not a showman.

But the real shift came when I asked, "Who needed to hear your message ten years ago?" She whispered, "Me."

And in that moment, her posture changed. She stopped trying to be confident. She became convicted. That emotion, her speaking to her former self, was the anchor. And that's what stuck.

## Ownership Cements It

Emotion opens the door. But ownership builds the house.

When someone experiences a shift in belief, it's fragile, like a young plant breaking through the soil. And if they see it as *your* idea, it stays external. The second someone challenges it, they'll let it go.

But when they feel like they came to it on their own—when they name it, personalize it, *claim* it—that's when it becomes durable. You've probably heard the phrase "people support what they help create." That's not just a feel-good leadership platitude. It's neuroscience.

Self-generated insights light up different regions of the brain, areas associated with memory, learning, and *intrinsic motivation*. Which means if you want the shift to last, don't just deliver it. Let them **discover** it.

Ask the question that lets them fill in the blank. Pause long enough for them to take the wheel. Reflect back what you heard and ask, "Is that true for you?" These are small moves, but they shift the dynamic from *influence* to *integration*.

One of the best examples I've ever seen came from a startup CEO I was advising. He wanted his team to stop waiting on him for every decision. But instead of issuing a policy or a demand, he walked into their Monday meeting and said: "Going forward, I want you to make every decision you can, as if I were out of the country and unreachable. What do you think that would look like?"

They sat up. They got curious. They debated. By the end of the meeting, they'd built their own framework. And because they *owned it*, they ran with it. The anchor wasn't the instruction, it was the **authorship**.

## Context Protects It

Let's say the emotional moment landed. Let's say they even took ownership. That's a win. But without reinforcement, even the strongest anchors erode over time.

The final principle is context.

We are always in motion. We go back into environments, teams, routines that pull us toward our default frames. Anchoring a new behavior means *embedding it into a space where it gets reinforced.*

That could mean creating a ritual. A visible cue. A shift in process or structure that makes the new belief easier to act on. Anchor lives best when it lives *somewhere*—a phrase, a hand signal, a whiteboard, a timestamp, a changed behavior that reminds them of the turning point.

One sales organization I worked with started closing every weekly standup with a "signal scan." Each rep would call out one signal they spotted that week and how they responded. It took five minutes. But it embedded the mindset. It turned signal-reading into culture, not just concept.

Context can also mean protecting the emotional stakes. A founder who reclaims her voice during coaching may need to record a voice memo right then, describing the shift. Later, when she wobbles, that memo isn't just a reminder. It's a **receipt**. It says, "You felt this. You earned this. Don't backslide."

We'll close this section with a personal moment from me. Here's a moment I've never forgotten and it's a perfect example of all three principles of anchoring at play.

I was running a workshop for a group of sales reps who were smart, gritty, emotionally aware, but stuck in one of those collective funks. The kind where you can't tell if it's fatigue, frustration, or fear, but you *know* it's blocking performance.

One of the reps, we'll call him Dave, was the quiet type. He was not disengaged, just reserved. You could tell he was smart, but he kept his distance during the exercises. When it came time to walk through a personal signal map (which, in STRATA terms, means identifying your own tells, triggers, and shifts), he sat back and said, "Honestly, I'm just tired of pretending. Clients say no and I act like it doesn't bother me. But it does."

He didn't expect to say that out loud. But when he did, the room went still. I asked him, "What happens if you stop pretending?"

He paused. He said, "Then I'd have to show up as someone who actually *gives a shit*. Not just play the game."

That line—*I'd have to show up as someone who gives a shit*—that became the anchor.

I had him write it on a card. The entire group adopted it. It became the rally cry for how they were going to pitch, handle objections, follow up, *everything*.

That one phrase—charged with emotion, owned by him, embedded in their team's culture—created a shift that stuck. Three months later, their VP emailed me: "Every time someone gets lazy or forgets why we're here, someone just says, 'Give a shit,' and the whole energy resets."

That's the power of a well-placed anchor. It takes something invisible and gives it form. Something felt, and gives it language. Something fleeting, and makes it permanent. To anchor something isn't to repeat it. It's to *root it*. It's the moment where your influence becomes architecture. Where you build memory around meaning.

Anchoring is the fourth layer in STRATA because it's the bridge between shift and sustainability. Without it, all the earlier steps—Signal, Trigger, Reframe—stay theoretical. They live in the moment but don't last beyond it.

But with it? You create beliefs that stick. You generate behaviors that recur. You change not just what people see but what they remember, *and who they believe they are because of it.*

Let's recap the three principles one more time:

- **Emotion seals it.** Without emotion, your insight evaporates. Anchor it with a moment they'll feel again.
- **Ownership cements it.** If it's yours, they'll debate it. If it's theirs, they'll defend it.
- **Context protects it.** Build anchors into their routines, space, language, or actions so the belief doesn't fade.

Remember, the goal of STRATA isn't to win a moment. It's to reshape a pattern. Anchoring is how you move from influence into impact. You've now moved someone. You've helped them see the signal. You've named the real trigger. You've reframed the narrative—and you've anchored the insight so it sticks.

But here's the final frontier: what happens *after*? What happens when you're no longer in the room? When you've coached the rep, or influenced the buyer, or had the hard conversation with your partner and now it's their turn to go out into the world and act on it?

That's where **Transfer** comes in.

The next layer of STRATA isn't about you at all. It's about how well the shift multiplies, how well they carry it forward, and whether the change you sparked becomes contagious, sustainable, *and scalable.*

In Chapter 6, we'll explore what it takes to build messages that replicate. Not just persuasion that works in the moment but influence that lives beyond you.

Let's turn the page. It's time to transfer the flame.

# CHAPTER 6

# TRANSFER — MAKE IT THEIRS

*"No one is ever truly convinced—they simply decide it was their idea all along."*

— Jake Stahl

*She said, "Interesting."*

*Then nothing changed.*

*Until you stopped explaining.*

*And asked, "If you were already doing this, how would you describe it to your team?"*

*She leaned forward.*

*And for the first time, you weren't talking to her.*

*She was talking to herself.*

## Transfer — Make It Theirs

If *Reframe* is the pivot, *Transfer* is the handoff. It's the moment when the shift you created doesn't just sit there between you, it moves. It lands. It roots. And most importantly… it becomes theirs.

It's the difference between convincing and aligning.

Up until now, you've been guiding the conversation, steering the emotional and psychological turns. You've recognized the signal. Named the trigger. Tilted the lens with a reframe. Anchored it emotionally. You've earned their attention. Maybe even their agreement. But agreement doesn't mean adoption. Agreement is a nod. Transfer is a grip.

If someone agrees with you but doesn't feel like the insight belongs to them, like they discovered it, like it clicked into place in their world, they're not taking it with them. They're admiring it from a distance. No matter how compelling your logic was or how sharp your reframe felt, if the belief doesn't make the shift from *your idea* to *their truth*, nothing sticks.

Transfer is where influence becomes internal.

A few years ago, I was consulting for a Fortune 500 sales team. This group was composed of smart people, plenty of experience, but they were completely underperforming in a new vertical. Leadership was frustrated. They had poured time, budget, and strategy into breaking into this space, but adoption was flat. Sales cycles were slow. No traction.

When I stepped in, I didn't overhaul the process. I didn't launch a new campaign. I sat in on ten sales calls. And on the third one, I saw it.

The rep was doing everything right... on paper. He'd positioned the offer clearly. Framed the problem. Used strong language. But every time the client asked a question, the rep responded like he was defending the material, not living it. Like he was presenting a framework, not solving a real-world problem. The client could feel it.

I stopped the tape, looked at the team, and said, "Tell me something. Do you believe this approach *actually* works for them?"

Silence. One rep finally said, "We know it works *in theory*. But we haven't seen it in the wild yet."

Exactly. That's a transfer problem.

They hadn't internalized the shift. They were still treating the approach like it belonged to someone else, something they were *told* to do, not something they'd claimed. So the client didn't feel conviction. They felt compliance. And no buyer moves on compliance.

Over the next two weeks, we didn't retrain the team, we *transferred* the mission. We got them to talk about how they'd use the new offer *themselves* if they were the client. We asked what part of the value prop *they* would bet on. We brought the solution out of the script and into their actual brain.

And just like that, everything changed. Calls went from hesitant to confident. Prospects stopped hesitating. The sales cycle shortened by 40%. Why? Because the belief wasn't being *taught* anymore, it was being *owned*.

That's the heartbeat of Transfer. Transfer happens when they hear themselves in it. There's a moment in every high-stakes conversation when the person across from you stops evaluating your idea... and starts trying it on.

They might not say it out loud, but you can feel the pause. The lean-in. The way their eyes flick up or they repeat something back under their breath. That's the quiet click of an idea becoming personal.

In STRATA, Transfer is the fifth layer because it *has to* come after anchoring. You can't transfer a concept that hasn't been emotionally validated. You can't hand someone a belief they haven't already started to feel. That's like trying to pass the baton before the runner's even moving.

So your job in Transfer is simple, but surgical: Make the belief feel familiar. Don't just say the right thing; say it in *their* language. Don't just drop insight; mirror their concern. Don't just deliver a solution; reveal that it was always in them. This is the moment where you're not the teacher. You're the trigger.

You're the switch that makes them think, *I've always known this...* *I just didn't have the words for it.* Now they do. And because they discovered it, because it was *theirs*, they'll fight for it.

A woman, let's call her Lauren, came to me during one of my live workshops. She was a VP of People for a fast-growing startup. She had a great team with incredible growth, but she was running herself into the ground trying to get buy-in from department heads on a new hiring philosophy.

"They all say they support it," she told me. "But no one actually changes anything. They still default to resumes and pedigree instead of potential. I've shown them the data. They nod their heads. Then go back to the old way."

This is a classic Transfer problem. I said, "What happens when you show them the data?"

She said, "I walk them through the metrics, the case studies, the ROI of hiring for agility."

"And what happens next?"

"They agree. Then nothing."

So I gave her a different play. "Next time you talk to them," I said, "ask one question. Just one. Say: 'Who was the best person you ever hired? And what made you take the chance on them?'"

She did. And it worked like a spell. Because every leader had a story. Every leader had a moment where they hired someone *without the pedigree* and watched them soar.

And as they told the stories, something shifted. They weren't defending the old method anymore, they were re-remembering their own instincts. By the end of the week, two departments had changed their job descriptions. Not because they were told to. But because they reclaimed the belief.

*They owned it.* That's Transfer.

## Three Rules of Transfer

Let's ground this in reality. Transfer isn't magic. It follows a structure:

1. **Make It Feel Like a Mirror, Not a Lesson.**

   People reject sermons. But they lean into stories that sound like their own. Let them feel like they've seen it before. Let the insight reflect back something they already suspected.

2. **Let Them Say It First (or Feel Like They Did).**

   When someone believes they discovered the truth, they'll defend it to the death. That's why your job is to leave breadcrumbs, not blueprints.

3. **Shift from Persuasion to Permission.**

   Stop trying to get a yes. Start creating space for one. When they feel like they're allowed to believe it, not forced to accept it, the resistance disappears.

Transfer doesn't always look loud. Sometimes it's subtle. It's the CFO who asks a question he already knows the answer to just to see if it still holds up under pressure. It's the founder who starts rewording your pitch in her own language before you're even done talking. It's the dad who sits quiet for three days after your conversation, then calls and says, "You know what? I think I've been thinking about this wrong."

Transfer is rarely a lightning bolt. It's a thaw. And that's why most people miss it. They're looking for the dramatic yes. The ah-ha moment. But Transfer is more like a hand slowly tightening around a truth that's always been there.

The moment Transfer is successful, you'll notice a few key signals:

- They start finishing your sentences.

- They start applying the idea to other areas you didn't even mention.
- They shift from listening mode to strategizing mode.

They don't need your permission anymore, they're already moving.

Let's go deeper.

Transfer isn't about being persuasive. It's about unlocking what they already suspect to be true. And that requires one powerful psychological principle most people miss: **Confirmation bias works both ways.**

Most people think of confirmation bias as a bad thing; people only hearing what supports what they already believe. But what if you could use it to your advantage? When you speak to someone in their language, reflect their worldview, and mirror back the truth already orbiting in their subconscious, confirmation bias becomes your ally.

You're not *changing* their mind; you're giving them permission to believe what they already wanted to believe. And that is the single fastest way to transfer ownership of an idea.

If someone secretly thinks they're being under-leveraged, and you say, "I think the most underused talent in this room is you," they don't argue. They absorb it. It feels like recognition, not persuasion. That idea sticks.

If someone already suspects the system is broken, and you say, "You're not imagining it, this setup rewards the wrong things," they lean in. Why? Because it confirms what they already felt in their gut but hadn't put into words yet.

Transfer is that internal sigh of relief that sounds like: *Finally, someone said it.* When done right, Transfer doesn't feel like a new idea. It feels like a remembered one. And that's the point.

## Why Transfer Comes Fifth in STRATA

STRATA is a system of movement. Psychological movement. Emotional movement. Decision-making movement.

You can't jump ahead. Each layer preps the next:

- **Signal** tells you what's real.
- **Trigger** shows you what's protected.
- **Reframe** shifts the angle.
- **Anchor** gives it emotional weight.
- **Transfer** makes it stick by making it theirs.

Only after all of that can you ask for **Action**.

Transfer is what protects the belief when you're not in the room. It's the difference between temporary compliance and lasting conviction.

Let me give you one more story. A few years ago, I was hired by a startup accelerator to work with a group of early-stage founders preparing for Demo Day. Each founder had three minutes to pitch investors. No pressure.

One of the founders, we'll call him Eli, was brilliant, technical, obsessive, and full of fire, but his pitch fell flat every time he practiced. Investors weren't getting it. Mentors were glazing over.

So I sat him down and said, "Tell me what made you start this company. No slides. No script. Just talk."

He said, "My sister. She has epilepsy. She was misdiagnosed twice and almost died before we found the right specialist. I built this platform to stop that from ever happening again." And there it was. The whole why. Sitting right there. Human, raw, unforgettable.

But none of that was in his pitch. He said, "I didn't want to make it about me."

I looked at him and said, "It's not about you. It's about giving them *permission* to care."

We rebuilt the pitch from that one thread. Instead of starting with the tech, he started with the story. And instead of laying out what the product *did*, he laid out the problem *he couldn't live with*. That gave investors a way in.

When he pitched at Demo Day, it was like watching the room breathe in sync. Eyes locked. Pens down. No phones out. He raised his round in three days. Because he didn't just transfer the idea. He transferred the *urgency*. He made them feel it, own it, and defend it. That's the ultimate goal. When the belief doesn't just stick—it spreads.

## And Now, a Word on Ego

Let's talk about the invisible enemy of Transfer: your ego.

It is *incredibly* tempting to want credit. To want to be the one who gave the insight, solved the problem, flipped the switch. Especially in high-stakes rooms or with resistant personalities, our instinct is to tighten our grip. To double down. To *prove* we're right.

But ego ruins Transfer. The moment someone senses that you're more attached to *being right* than to *getting it right*, they pull away. Because now it feels like a competition, not a collaboration.

Remember: they don't have to *thank* you. They have to *own* it. If you walk out of the room and they quote you to their team without saying your name? That's a win. If they argue your point passionately next week as if it was their own idea? That's Transfer.

Don't steal it back with your need to be recognized. Let them have it. Let them wear it. Let them claim it. Because the second they do, you're done. You did your job. And now you can move on to the final step.

Transfer creates the conditions for movement. But movement still needs a door. That's where Action lives. Because insight without action is just intellectual clutter, belief without behavior changes nothing, and Transfer without momentum becomes a forgotten feeling.

In Chapter 7, we'll break down exactly how to *move the moment* from agreement to action. Not by pushing. But by positioning the next step so clearly, so naturally, and so powerfully that it feels like *the only thing left to do*. That's what great influence is. It's not about pressure. It's about precision and you're ready for it.

Let's go get it.

# CHAPTER 7

# ACTION — TURN BELIEF INTO BEHAVIOR

*"Vision without action is a daydream. Action without vision is a nightmare."*

— Japanese Proverb

*He didn't need more proof.*

*He didn't need more time.*

*He just sat there, hands flat on the table, like the decision had already been made.*

*And then he said,*

*"Alright... what happens next?"*

*Because belief isn't the finish line.*

*It's the starting gun.*

## Action — Turn Belief into Behavior

You can do everything right. Read the signal. Name the trigger. Reframe the moment. Anchor it. Transfer the belief. But if they don't act? You've got influence with no impact. Action is where it all lands… or dies.

Action is the final layer of STRATA. Not because it's the end of the journey. But because it's the moment the journey turns into motion. Without it, you're not a strategist. You're a storyteller. A powerful one, maybe. But stories that don't move people are just background noise.

The world is full of people who've been inspired but unchanged. Fired up but unmoved. Told exactly what they need to hear, and still… stuck.

Action is what cuts through that. And here's the first hard truth:

**Action is not a finish line. It's a doorway.** We're not looking for compliance. We're not demanding obedience. This isn't about pressure. STRATA has never been about forcing, it's always been about *freeing*. Helping someone move not because you said so, but because the next step became *inevitable*.

So when we talk about Action in STRATA, we're talking about something very specific: The behavior that naturally emerges once belief is internalized, emotion is anchored, and the path is clear. It's not about pushing people. It's about removing the reasons they wouldn't move. Let me show you how this works.

A few years ago, I was coaching a regional sales director for a pharmaceutical company. He was a brilliant guy, charismatic, but his numbers had plateaued. His team liked him, but they weren't moving. Every initiative felt like a chore. Every new process got polite agreement, and then… silence.

He came to me frustrated. "I know what needs to happen. I've told them a hundred times. Why aren't they doing it?"

I asked him a question: "When was the last time you made it easy for someone to say yes?"

He blinked. "What do you mean?"

I said, "They believe you. They trust you. But you're giving them too much to chew at once. You're handing them a buffet and expecting a bite. They're overwhelmed. Not unmotivated."

So we changed one thing. Instead of rolling out new processes in big quarterly meetings, he started creating micro-asks. One step at a time. One action per week. Always tied to a why, always tied to a win. He used the language we shaped together, language that *sounded* like his people, not corporate speak, not mandates.

"Try this one shift in how you open your next call, and see what happens." It worked.

The team didn't just perform. They *surprised* him. Because action, when it's designed right, doesn't just create results. It creates *momentum*.

Here's what most people get wrong about behavior: They think it's about *motivation*. But motivation is a feeling. Behavior is a function of clarity and context. If the action isn't obvious, safe, and meaningful, it won't happen.

And this is where STRATA earns its name. Each layer before this has been clearing space. Getting you closer. Peeling back the resistance. So by the time you hit Action, you're not launching a campaign. You're lighting a fuse.

Let me break this down.

## The Psychology of Action

Action isn't a single moment. It's a progression. There's a behavioral psychology principle called the "intention-behavior gap." It's the space between *wanting* to do something and *actually* doing it.

Most ideas die in that space. So the job of a behavioral strategist—your job now—is to collapse that gap. To make it smaller. Easier. Stickier.

There are three principles that drive this:

1. **Clarity reduces hesitation.**
2. **Emotion drives initiation.**
3. **Micro-commitments create traction.**

Let's hit each one in real-world terms.

## 1. Clarity reduces hesitation.

When people hesitate, they're not rejecting your idea, they're stalling because the next step isn't obvious. If you want someone to act, you have to show them *what that action looks like.*

Not in five steps. Not in a full-blown plan. Just one move.

The clearest action is the one that can be done *now*, without approval, without budget, without permission. If it requires buy-in from five people, it's not an action, it's a proposal. If it requires a shift in mindset, that's still Transfer. But if it's something they can do today, right now, then you've landed the plane.

## 2. Emotion drives initiation.

Belief fuels change, but emotion starts the engine. If someone *feels* like they're on the edge of something important, they're more likely to lean in. Think about it like this: every decision has a tipping point. Logic stacks the reasons. But emotion is what leans the chair.

That's why STRATA layers matter so much.

-Signal gives you the read.

-Trigger opens the door.

-Reframe changes the story.

-Anchor makes it stick.

-Transfer makes it theirs.

But *Action*? Action asks: "What now?"

And that question only gets answered if emotion is still alive in the room. You don't need fireworks. But you *do* need to feel the moment.

## 3. Micro-commitments create traction.

Here's the real killer of momentum: *ambition overload.* You ask for too much. You make it too complex. You try to change everything at once. And people freeze.

The best way to avoid that? Ask for a *micro-yes*. A reply. A comment. A short list. A signal back. Give them something small, but real. Something visible. Because once someone says yes to *anything*, they're more likely to say yes again. It's behavioral momentum.

Want a practical example? A friend of mine was trying to help his teenage son get out of a rut. The kid was smart, but withdrawn. He wasn't doing homework, wasn't socializing, just skating by.

Lectures didn't work. Therapy didn't land. So one night, my friend just said to his son, "Hey, would you help me research speakers for a talk I'm giving?" There was no pressure. No expectation. Just involvement. And the kid said yes.

He dove into the research. Started asking questions. Got curious. That little yes cracked the shell. It led to a second ask. Then a third. A new rhythm. That's the anatomy of Action. It's not a battle cry. It's a breadcrumb trail. You don't need them to sprint. You just need them to *step*.

That's the part most people don't get: *change doesn't require a leap.* It starts with the smallest possible movement that feels safe, real, and theirs. If Transfer is the emotional adoption of an idea, Action is its physical expression.

But here's where things get even more powerful:

## Action teaches belief.

Yes, you read that right. We often assume belief must come first and behavior follows. But the inverse is also true; sometimes behavior *creates* belief.

There's an old principle in psychology called *self-perception theory*. It basically says: we infer our beliefs by observing our behavior. If I act brave, I must be brave. If I step up, maybe I *am* the kind of person who steps up.

You don't have to convince someone to believe in themselves. You just need them to *do something* they didn't think they could do and let the belief catch up.

That's how STRATA accelerates momentum: by designing moments where the action teaches the identity.

## Identity follows behavior.

Want someone to think of themselves as a leader? Give them a leadership moment. Want them to see themselves as a closer, a risk-taker, a creative force? Give them the *smallest act* of closure, risk, or creation. One they can win.

And when they do, don't say "See, I told you so." Say: "That's who you've been the whole time." You're not giving them power. You're naming what was already there. That's STRATA.

Now let's talk friction. Because even when everything is right—even when the belief is strong, the emotion is present, and the step is clear—there will *still* be resistance.

Here's why:

## People don't fear the action itself. They fear what the action will cost them.

Will it cost them status? Certainty? Comfort? Control?

The behavior isn't the problem. The *meaning* of the behavior is. Saying "I need help" feels like weakness. Changing direction feels like failure. Taking a leap feels like risk.

Your job in STRATA is to neutralize the cost.

You can do that in two ways:

1.  **Redefine the action.**

    You shift the meaning. Saying "I need help" becomes "I'm ready to move faster." Changing direction becomes "I've outgrown the old map." Taking a leap becomes "I'm trusting myself more than my fear."

2.  **Widen the lens.**

    You show them what *not* acting will cost them. Not as a scare tactic, but as a gentle mirror. You reflect what staying here *really means*.

Because once someone sees that staying stuck is riskier than moving forward, they'll move.

There was a woman in one of my workshops. We'll call her Dana. She was in her mid-40s, mid-career, and razor sharp. She had all the markers of success... but had been sitting on an idea for years—a coaching business. This was something deeply personal to her, but she never launched it. She kept saying, "It's not the right time."

I sat with her during a break and asked her what the actual fear was. She said, "I don't want to look stupid."

I nodded. Then said: "What would be worse, looking stupid for five minutes, or looking back in five years and realizing you never tried?"

She didn't say anything at first. Then she whispered, "That second one. That's worse."

That was it. That was the shift. By the end of that month, she had a landing page up, a beta group signed, and her first three clients. Not because I gave her a strategy but because I made the *action* cost less than the alternative.

That's STRATA in motion.

Now let's bring it home:


## How do you design action in a way that's real, repeatable, and rooted in behavior?

You follow the Five R's.

These are your tools. Use them anytime you need to convert belief into behavior.

1. **Reveal**

   Make the invisible cost of *inaction* clear.

2. **Reframe**

   Shift the meaning of the step so it aligns with who they already believe they are.

3. **Reduce**

   Break the action into the smallest possible commitment that still counts.

4. **Reward**

   Acknowledge and celebrate the shift, no matter how small. This isn't about praise; it's about reinforcement. The brain needs to know: *this was a win.*

5. **Repeat**

   Set the stage for a second, slightly bigger step. That's how patterns form. One step is a shift. Two steps is momentum. Three? That's identity.

So when you walk into a room to a pitch a hard conversation, this is your job:

Read the room.

Name what's hiding.

Flip the lens.

Make it real.

Let them own it.

And *move them.*

That's STRATA.

And this final step—Action—isn't just a close. It's a beginning. It's the doorway into the future. The one you helped them see, feel, claim... and now walk toward. Not because you sold them. But because you *set them free.*

So wherever you go next, whatever room, stage, negotiation, or moment you step into, remember this: Influence isn't about being the loudest voice in the room. It's about being the *clearest path forward.* Let's make it count.

# CHAPTER 8

# STRATA IN RELATIONSHIPS

*"The most important thing in communication is hearing what isn't said."*

— Peter Drucker

*She swore she was fine.*

*Said it with a smile.*

*But her eyes flicked to the floor,*

*and her voice landed just a half-step too late.*

*You didn't need to hear the words.*

*You'd already heard the truth.*

## STRATA in Relationships

The first time I realized STRATA wasn't just for boardrooms or sales calls, I was sitting across the table from my daughter. She was thirteen. She was bright, self-protective, quick with sarcasm, a mirror of myself in ways that scared the hell out of me. We were mid-conversation about her grades. I was doing what most parents do: asking questions that sounded like I cared, but really were just veiled attempts at control. She was doing what most teenagers do: nodding, shrugging, letting her body speak louder than her voice.

And then she did something small—so small I almost missed it. She reached for her water, but didn't drink it. Just held it. Her gaze dropped to the table. Her foot tapped once.

Trigger.

I stopped talking. That pause changed everything. Because in that second, I wasn't her dad trying to fix a situation. I was a man trying to read a room. And that room just happened to be my own daughter's nervous system. I had triggered something—not overt, not dramatic, but real. Maybe a sense of being judged. Maybe the memory of a past lecture. Maybe just the fear of disappointing me again.

It doesn't matter what the origin was. What mattered was that I *saw* it. And in seeing it, I made a different move. "Hey," I said, quieter now. "You don't have to answer that. We can just sit." She nodded, still not looking at me. But the foot stopped tapping.

We sat for a minute. Then she said, "It's not the grades. It's that I feel stupid in math. I just don't get it."

That moment didn't come from parenting techniques. It didn't come from active listening strategies or therapeutic mirroring. It came from STRATA. From the signal I noticed, the trigger I honored, the reframe I *didn't* force, and the anchor I offered by staying present instead of persuasive.

I learned that day what I now teach every client I work with: STRATA is not just a system for influence. It's a system for intimacy. Intimacy isn't built on truth. It's built on safety. And safety lives in how we respond to each other's signals, especially when the stakes are high and the conversations are charged.

Let's rewind to the start of most relationship breakdowns. The breakdown usually doesn't begin with betrayal or anger; it begins with missed signals. A flinch you didn't catch. A tone that went unchecked. A rhythm you didn't notice had changed. One person leans out, subtly. The other doesn't notice, or worse, takes it personally and leans harder. The conversation becomes layered. Defensive. Dense. And just like that, you're not talking to each other anymore. You're talking to the *idea* of each other. To the role. The story. The projection.

This happens in marriages. In families. In deep friendships. And it always follows the same pattern:

The signal gets missed.

The trigger gets pushed.

The reframe doesn't happen.

The anchor slips.

The transfer stalls.

And the action becomes withdrawal.

When I started applying STRATA to my own marriage, the first thing I noticed was how often I'd been trying to *win* instead of trying to *see*. My wife's signals weren't mysterious. I was just too caught in my own momentum to read them. The look she gave when I walked in talking too fast. The silence she offered when I shared an idea but didn't ask her what she thought. The one-word answers. The polite smile. These weren't surface behaviors. They were messages. And I was missing every one of them. It wasn't that she didn't want to connect. It was that I wasn't *reachable* in the moment I most needed to be.

One night, after a particularly long week, I came home excited about something I had just launched. I talked for ten straight minutes. She nodded, smiled, said all the right things. But something in her body said otherwise.

Her shoulders were higher than usual. Her mouth stayed tight when she smiled. Her nods were just a little too rhythmic like a metronome of agreement rather than true engagement. This was signal mismatch.

I stopped mid-sentence. "You seem quiet," I said.

She exhaled. Slowly. Not frustrated. Just tired. "I want to hear all of this," she said, "but I need a minute. I just walked through the door, and I feel like I'm already behind."

Old me would've felt rejected. Shut down. Disrespected. STRATA-trained me. I saw it for what it was: a boundary wrapped in kindness. A request for recalibration. So I pivoted. I anchored to her world instead of mine. "Totally fair," I said. "I'll heat up dinner and give you space. Just let me know when you're ready to dive in."

Ten minutes later, we were laughing. Connected. Talking for real. That moment didn't happen because I was being a "good husband." It happened because I honored the *signal*. Because I noticed the *trigger*. Because I chose not to push through with performance.

You want to fix your relationships? Learn to *stop performing*. Performing is what we do when we don't feel safe being seen. And that's what most relational breakdowns come down to: two people performing the roles they think will preserve the connection, instead of showing up as the versions that might actually repair it.

Let me give you a story about a coaching client. We'll call her Elise. She was a founder, type-A, sharp as hell, and terrified of being misunderstood. She came to me for executive presence training. What she ended up getting was a relationship intervention.

About a month in, she said, "My partner keeps saying he doesn't feel heard. But I listen. I validate. I even repeat back what he says."

I asked her to describe their last argument.

"We were talking about finances. He said he felt like I didn't include him in the big decisions. I told him that wasn't true. I walked him through every step I took."

I said, "And what did his body do when you started explaining?"

She paused. "He looked away. Crossed his arms."

"Signal," I said.

She nodded slowly. "I didn't catch it. I thought he was just shutting down."

"He was," I said. "Because you were proving a fact instead of reading a fear."

We roleplayed it. I had her repeat the conversation, but this time, notice the moment his posture shifted. When she saw it, I had her stop.

"Now," I said, "don't explain. Just name it. Gently."

She said, "I saw you look away just now. Did that hit wrong?"

I played the partner: "I guess it did. I just feel like every time I bring something up, you turn it into a debate."

Elise went quiet. Her eyes softened. "I do that," she said. "Because I think if I can make you see I'm right, you won't leave."

And just like that, the real conversation started. That's STRATA in relationships. Not a script. Not a strategy. A *lens*. A commitment to tracking the moment instead of trying to control the outcome.

Most people don't need you to be right. They need you to be reachable. Reachability is the currency of intimacy. And STRATA, when used well, makes you reachable without making you weak.

You don't collapse your signal. You tune it.

You don't avoid the trigger. You hold space for it.

You don't rush the reframe. You wait for the real moment.

You don't anchor to logic. You anchor to *felt truth*.

You don't transfer ownership by force. You hand it over with presence.

Let me show you one more version of STRATA in relationships that most people overlook: *repair*. This is the art of making it right when you've already gotten it wrong. Most people bungle this. They apologize with performance.

"I'm sorry you feel that way," "That wasn't my intention," "I didn't mean to make you upset." These statements sound good. They feel responsible. But they don't land.

Why? Because they bypass the *signal*. They ignore the *trigger*. They try to skip to the end—*action* and *closure* without doing the emotional work of alignment. I once hurt someone I care deeply about with a careless comment. I thought I was being playful. They experienced it as dismissive. Days passed. The space grew. When I finally got the courage to reach out, I didn't start with my defense. I started with STRATA.

"When I said what I said, I saw your body shift. You smiled, but it didn't reach your eyes. And then you went quiet. I kept talking like nothing happened, and I shouldn't have. That moment deserved attention. I'm sorry for missing it. I'd like to understand what it felt like from your side."

They replied within ten minutes. Not because the words were perfect. But because I had read the signal correctly. That's what STRATA gives you. Not control. Not eloquence. But *accuracy*. And when you're accurate in relationships, even broken ones can reopen. And that's where we go next. Because there's one final layer we haven't touched yet: the relationship you have with yourself.

Most people try to fix their relationships by working on the other person. They think, "If they would just listen more. If they'd stop reacting. If they could just be a little more self-aware." But STRATA doesn't start with someone else; it starts with presence. And the hardest presence to sit with is your own.

When you get reactive in a relationship—when you over-talk, defend, collapse, or retreat—those aren't random habits, they're strategies your nervous system adopted to protect you. They once served a purpose, and now, they're outdated software running in the background of your life.

The work, then, is not to shame the strategy. It's to recognize the signal underneath it. Why did I feel the need to explain that? Why did I raise my voice? Why did I shut down?

These aren't questions to guilt yourself with. They're questions to *map* with STRATA.

What signal did I miss?

What trigger got hit?

What reframe didn't happen?

When you start mapping your own moments like this, you stop blaming and start building. You begin to notice when your partner's silence mirrors your own fear of inadequacy. When their criticism mirrors your inner self-talk. When their withdrawal is less about you and more about a lifetime of not knowing how to ask for closeness.

You realize: most relationship pain isn't personal. It's *patterned*. And STRATA gives you the lens to see the pattern instead of reacting to the person.

That's the real magic of STRATA in relationships. Not that it helps you communicate better, though it does. Not that it makes you more emotionally intelligent, though it will. But because it gives you a way to see beneath the moment. To track what's really going on, without needing the other person to tell you.

When someone says "I'm fine" but everything about their body says otherwise...

Because when someone says "You never listen" but what they really mean is "I don't feel safe saying what I want..."

Because when someone leaves and you say "They abandoned me," but the real story is "I abandoned myself long before they did..."

That's where STRATA lives. Not in the words. In the *moment beneath the words*. And when you learn to read that moment in yourself, in them, in the space between, you don't just become better at relationships. You become impossible to fake it with. And that is a kind of intimacy this world is starving for.

# CHAPTER 9

# READING THE ROOM

*"The room is always talking. Most people just aren't listening."*

— Unknown

*He didn't flinch.*

*Didn't frown.*

*Just tapped his pen—*

*once—*

*and the room went quiet.*

*The meeting went on,*

*but the verdict was already in.*

## Reading the Room

There's a moment in every high-stakes room where time seems to stretch. The words stop mattering. The pitch is still happening, the presentation still flowing, but beneath it all, the room is deciding something else entirely: *Do we trust you? Are you worth listening to? Are you reading us, or just reading your notes?*

And if you miss that moment. If you're locked in on what you rehearsed instead of what the room is showing you, you don't just lose attention. You lose *permission.*

That's what makes group dynamics so slippery. It's not just one person's signals you're tracking. It's a dozen overlapping agendas, egos, energy shifts, and silent power structures, all colliding in real time. And what worked in a one-on-one conversation can fall flat, or worse backfire, when multiple people are watching, waiting, and testing how you respond under group pressure.

STRATA wasn't built just for solo influence. It was built for this: the group room. The pitch meeting with five stakeholders. The executive table where alliances form before you arrive. The family intervention that's already rehearsed its verdict. The hospital committee debating access. The keynote crowd you can feel slipping away.

This is where *reading* the room becomes *steering* the room. And if you want that level of command—not performance, but traction— you need to treat the room like a system, not a scene, because in any group setting, you're not speaking to one audience. You're speaking to three at once:

1. **The dominant signal:** the person or people setting the emotional tone for the room.
2. **The resistant signal:** the person quietly (or loudly) withholding buy-in.
3. **The watching signal:** the observers deciding who to align with based on how the tension unfolds.

The mistake most people make is trying to win the room as if it's a single unit. But STRATA teaches you to *triangulate,* to locate the center of gravity, the silent blockers, and the permission holders. That's how you earn the room's attention without chasing it.

Let's start with the **dominant signal.**

This is the person most others take unconscious cues from. They may not say the most but when they shift posture, others follow. When they look skeptical, the group tilts toward doubt. When they lean in, people start listening harder. They're not always the highest-ranking person. Sometimes it's the emotional center of the team. Sometimes it's the skeptic everyone respects. But in every room, there's someone anchoring the tone. And your first job is to find them.

Watch where eyes go during small talk. Who people check in with before agreeing. Who stays still when others adjust. These micro-cues point you to the signal setter. And once you find them, STRATA says: calibrate to *them first*. Not to please, but to earn neutrality.

If you skip the dominant signal and focus on friendlier faces, the room fragments. You get smiles, nods, even compliments but no real momentum. The energy never consolidates, and you walk out feeling like it went well, only to be ghosted later. That's a misread.

Now to the **resistant signal**.

This is the person testing you. The one giving cold eyes or disengaged body language. Sometimes they challenge you out loud. Sometimes they sit silently, arms crossed, waiting for you to slip. And the reflex most people have is to avoid them. To win over the agreeable ones instead. But that's not how posture works in a group.

Avoidance sends a signal. When you skip the resistant person. When you don't look at them, don't respond directly, don't meet their energy, you confirm their doubts. You telegraph that they hold the power. And now *they* become the unspoken leader of the room, whether they want to or not.

STRATA says: don't over-cater to resistance, but don't ignore it either. Address it without fear. Acknowledge concerns early. Ask them a sharp, neutral question. Look them in the eye when you make your most grounded point. This doesn't have to be confrontational. It has to be real. Posture meets posture. That's how you disarm tension without dancing for approval.

And finally: the **watching signal**.

This is the rest of the room, the people reading *you* based on how you handle the others. They're not sure yet. They're observing. Looking for signs. Is this person adaptable? Confident? Rattled? Over-rehearsed? Are they picking up on what's happening or steamrolling with their own agenda?

You can't fake presence with them. You have to earn it. And that happens not just through content, but through calibration. The watching signal doesn't respond to pitch polish. It responds to behavioral fluency. Can you read the shift in tone when someone checks their phone? Can you pause when you lose them, then re-engage with a story that lands? Can you name what's happening without blaming anyone?

That's STRATA in the group room. Not control. Not charm. *Calibration.*

Let's get concrete. Imagine you're in front of a buying committee. There are six people on Zoom, half of the cameras on, faces mostly blank. You open with your elevator pitch. No one interrupts, but no one smiles. One woman shifts in her seat when you mention personalization. Another man squints and leans back when you talk about integration. The senior leader looks down the whole time.

Most people would barrel ahead, maybe ask, "Any questions so far?" and plow into a demo. But STRATA says: pause. Track. Decode. Re-enter.

The woman who shifted? That's a signal. You circle back with: "When I mentioned customization, I noticed some engagement. Is that a pain point you've run into?" She leans forward. Starts talking. Now others turn their cameras on. You've unlocked the thread. You keep the attention not by moving forward, but by anchoring back.

Now the man who squinted? That's resistance. You don't confront him, but you say, "I know integration has burned a lot of teams in the past. Want to unpack how we approach it differently?" He nods just slightly but the tension drops.

That's STRATA in the group room. Not pitching louder. Reading deeper. The room isn't one entity. It's a constellation. And every person is either a source of signal, or an amplifier of someone else's. If you walk in with a fixed plan, you lose. But if you walk in trained to read heat, posture, micro-movements, and energy shifts, you don't just survive group settings. You start bending them.

The most powerful people in a room aren't always the ones talking the most. More often, they're the ones whose influence is felt in the silences, in the subtle reactions that ripple outward, even when no one else notices. A head tilt. A shift in breath. A stillness that spreads across the room like a quiet command.

When you're fluent in STRATA, you start to notice these shifts not as background noise, but as directional cues. The room is constantly broadcasting its state, what it's defending, what it's hesitant about, where it's drawn, and what it's begging someone to name. Most people miss these moments because they're focused on delivery. But STRATA practitioners don't just speak, they listen to what's not being said and let the room shape what comes next.

Consider what happens when you step on stage in front of a live audience. Maybe it's right after lunch. The crowd is scattered, a little heavy, faces lit by phone screens instead of stage lights. You weren't the act they came to see. You weren't promised. And now the air is thick with that low-grade resistance that makes most speakers rush.

This is the make-or-break moment. The standard approach is to spike energy, to throw in humor, crank the volume, or lean into a practiced opener designed to jolt the crowd awake. But STRATA tells you to do something radically different: slow down. Match not the expected pattern, but the actual signal.

If the room is flat, don't meet it with artificial hype. Drop into presence. Breathe. Speak with measured clarity. Tell a story that opens a question, not a demand. When you do this right—when you tune into the room instead of trying to override it, something subtle happens. Heads lift.

Phones go dark. Breathing syncs. You've created micro-alignment by honoring the moment, not escaping it.

That's when the room starts to shift, not because you forced it, but because you *met* it. That moment of alignment opens the gate to the rest of the STRATA framework. You're now in a position to build, not just speak. You start making choices not based on your outline, but based on readiness.

Here's how that plays out behaviorally.

- **Signal** is the read. "Where are they, really?"
- **Trigger** is the disruption. "What moment jolts them awake?"
- **Reframe** is the lens shift. "Can they see this differently now?"
- **Anchor** is the gut hit. "What's the phrase or story that will *stick*?"
- **Transfer** is the handoff. "What can they try for themselves, right now?"
- **Action** is the ask. "What are they now prepared to do, because of this arc?"

You don't fire these off like a checklist. You deploy them like architecture. Every STRATA layer is structural. It's how you design influence without guessing. You build the arc of the presentation, conversation, or negotiation with behavioral intention, not just content order.

Now zoom out and imagine a different kind of group room: a family intervention. There are four siblings in a living room. One of them is spiraling. He's drinking too much, isolating, self-sabotaging. The family has gathered to intervene, but from the second the conversation starts, the room ignites. The spiral sibling is silent, but you can feel the temperature spike. One brother starts talking too loudly, too quickly, trying to control the narrative. Another sibling tears up. The energy fractures. Everyone is reacting, but no one is aligned.

In STRATA, this isn't chaos, it's choreography. It's a group dynamic waiting to be read. The brother who's ranting? He's the dominant signal. He controls the heat. The spiral sibling, withdrawn and unresponsive, is the resistant signal, the one withholding permission. And the others? They're watching, waiting to see how power and pressure get redistributed.

If you charge into this moment with logic or tactics, you'll break the frame. But if you anchor your posture physically, emotionally, and behaviorally, you can start to guide. You drop your voice. You slow your breath. And you name what's happening without exaggerating it:

"I know this feels messy. No one wants to be here. And it's easy to feel like we're all ganging up. But we wouldn't be here if we didn't care enough to try."

That's the Reframe. You didn't deny the tension. You gave it a home. Now you Trigger a shift: "I want to ask something different. Not, 'What's wrong with you?' But, 'What's hard for you right now that none of us have seen?'"

You didn't ask for vulnerability. You created conditions for it. And when you do this? The dominant signal, the brother, may lower his volume. The resistant signal may shift in their seat or glance up. The watching signals start leaning in. The room hasn't been fixed. But it's now moving together. And *that* is alignment. Not agreement. Not harmony. *Alignment.*

The same approach works in high-stakes sales. You're in a pitch meeting. The CEO is leaning back, arms crossed. He hasn't said a word. The CFO is grilling you on margins. The VP of Operations is nodding but hasn't spoken. It's a split room, and every person is broadcasting a different channel.

STRATA trains you to read not the words, but the weight of posture. The CEO is dominant, but withholding. That's a flag. The CFO is resistant, but talking. That's leverage. The VP is watching, ready to be tipped either way. Most salespeople would keep pushing their slide deck, hoping the numbers will land.

But a STRATA practitioner narrows the aperture. You don't pitch harder. You say: "What we're hearing from teams your size isn't that they need more options. It's that they need *one* that doesn't break when the pressure hits. I'm guessing that's part of why we're here."

Now you've disrupted the emotional choreography. The CEO blinks. The CFO leans back. The VP tilts forward. You haven't closed the deal. But you've opened the door, because what you just did wasn't persuasion, it was *precision*.

Here's the brutal truth STRATA exposes: most people present to groups. STRATA teaches you to *converse* with them even when no one speaks.

Groups don't speak in sentences. They speak in glances, gestures, shifts in rhythm. When someone raises an eyebrow during your pitch, they're not just confused, they're signaling friction. When two people exchange a glance after you make a point, they're aligning or dividing. When a room goes totally still, you've either hit something true... or something dangerous. STRATA helps you know the difference.

In the group room, your content is never enough. Your radar is what matters. The best group leaders aren't the most charismatic. They're the most calibrated. They don't perform certainty. They scan tension. They pivot before the room breaks. They track who's holding resistance and who's silently begging for someone to lead.

And that's the real promise of STRATA in the group room: not to win approval, but to earn alignment. At scale. In real time. Without selling yourself out just to be heard.

# CHAPTER 10

# THE INNER CONVERSATION

*"Your mind is a battlefield where you are both armies."*

— Unknown

*You smiled.*

*Agreed.*

*Even leaned in.*

*But behind your eyes,*

*the debate was already raging—*

*and the loudest voice*

*wasn't theirs.*

## The Inner Conversation

Before you ever open your mouth in a room, a conversation has already started. Not with the client. Not with your partner. Not with the team. With yourself.

And if you don't know how to read that conversation. If you haven't trained yourself to track its signals, its spirals, its sudden shifts in energy, you will walk into every high-stakes moment already following a script you didn't choose. The tension you bring, the assumptions you project, the posture that leaks. None of it begins in the room. It begins in the invisible narrative underneath your breath.

The most persuasive person in your life is always you. You are persuading yourself all day long. To speak. To stay quiet. To go for it. To retreat. To double down. To abandon the plan. To armor up. To prove it. To pretend you don't care. And it's all happening faster than thought. This isn't some abstract concept. This is real-time nervous system strategy. And if you've ever walked out of a meeting thinking, "Why did I just say that?" or "Why did I play small?" you've already seen how fast that inner conversation can hijack the outer one.

That's why STRATA isn't just an external influence system. It's an internal awareness system. It's built to help you decode your own psychology before you project it onto the world around you. Most influence models are focused on output. STRATA starts upstream, at the input level where the emotional current begins.

Let's say someone questions your expertise in a meeting. In real time, what happens? Your face goes hot. Your body tenses. Your mind pulls a memory from a similar moment ten years ago. Without realizing it, your tone sharpens. You lean away. You start speaking faster. You add detail that wasn't needed. And suddenly, the moment is no longer about this conversation, it's about protecting yourself from something older.

That's what happens when the inner conversation goes unchecked. And if you've spent your whole career learning how to control the room without learning how to read your own signal, this will feel like a blind spot you never trained for.

But here's the truth: most people don't need new words. They need a better signal read of what they're already believing. That's the real leverage. Not changing the sentence. Changing the state it comes from.

STRATA breaks this down layer by layer.

**Signal:** What is your body trying to say before your brain can catch up? Are your shoulders curling in? Are your hands going cold? Is your breath short? These aren't just symptoms, they're stories. Your system is signaling something about safety, perception, or readiness. Before you try to override it, you need to decode it. This is where most people fail: they try to "perform" over a signal they haven't interpreted. That always leaks.

**Trigger:** What memory is being activated? What relational pattern is playing out? Did someone's tone remind you of a parent, a boss, a bully? The brain doesn't distinguish between current events and past experiences, it responds to *pattern similarity*. That means you're not always reacting to the person in front of you. You're reacting to who they *feel like*. And that reaction can cloud everything unless it's interrupted.

**Reframe:** What's another equally plausible interpretation of this moment? Reframing isn't about being delusional. It's about opening up your behavioral aperture. If the current belief makes you shrink, withdraw, attack, or please, it's probably not the most strategic frame. A strong reframe is grounded in truth *and* expansion. It doesn't ask, "Is this right?" It asks, "What else could be true that gives me better options?"

**Anchor:** What do you know to be true, regardless of this moment's noise? An anchor is not a pep talk. It's a felt truth. Something in your body that says, "I've been here before. I've handled worse. I know who I am." It could be a phrase. A breath. A memory of competence. A win you earned. A moment when you stood your ground. The anchor is how you regulate your internal posture when the external world starts to spin.

**Transfer:** Now that you've decoded the signal, recognized the trigger, reframed the moment, and rooted yourself in truth, what are you *giving yourself permission* to do? Speak up? Take a beat? Say no? Ask a question you'd normally avoid? Transfer is about translating inner clarity into outer action. Without it, all the inner work just floats.

**Action:** This is the only part anyone else sees. But by the time you get here, the game is already won or lost. Action is where your signal either leaks or lands. If it comes from coherence, you speak with gravity. If it comes from confusion, you speak with noise.

Let's make this concrete. You're in a negotiation. The stakes are high. You've rehearsed. You've strategized. You've role-played. But when they push back hard, you flinch. You say, "We can be flexible." You hear yourself say it, and you regret it instantly. Why? Because you didn't lose clarity in that moment. You lost *access* to it.

The inner conversation, already primed with fear of being too rigid, fear of losing the deal, fear of being seen as difficult, had already decided the posture. Your body executed what your brain hadn't finished thinking through. That's how fast the inner loop works. And that's why it must be trained on the front end, not the back.

STRATA is not a feel-good system. It's not built for performance. It's built for calibration. And there's nothing that needs tighter calibration than the stories you tell yourself in the first five seconds of tension. Because you're not just telling those stories, you're *acting* from them. And people feel it. They don't just hear your pitch. They *feel* whether you believe yourself. They feel whether your posture matches your promise. They feel whether the words you're saying are coming from a place of alignment or compensation.

Here's where things shift: when you learn to *observe* your inner conversation in real time, it no longer drives you. It becomes data, not destiny. That's how you begin to detach. Not by numbing out, but by noticing. When you can catch the sentence before it finishes, "They're not going to take me seriously," and pause long enough to ask, "Is that mine, or is that old?" you reclaim the wheel.

When you start responding to the moment in front of you, rather than the ghost of a moment from years ago, you speak with authority. Not because you're faking confidence, but because you've returned to the present.

Let's walk it into daily life. You're on the receiving end of critique from someone you admire. Maybe it's fair. Maybe it stings. Either way, it lands in that place where you start to shrink. You hear, *You didn't think this through.* But your inner conversation turns it into, *You're not smart enough. You're not strategic. You're always behind.* The body doesn't differentiate between feedback and shame. It hears the tone, reads the posture, and replays whatever memory fits.

But this time, you pause. You feel the contraction. The tight chest. The drop in energy. You don't flinch or fight. You recognize the pattern. Signal detected.

Now you run STRATA inside, mid-moment.

**What's the trigger?** This reminds you of your dad's disappointment when you failed a test at twelve. The same look. The same sigh. You've carried that with you for decades. No wonder this feels heavier than it is.

**Reframe:** This isn't about your worth. This is a moment of adjustment. A professional offering an insight. Their feedback doesn't make you less. It gives you a tool.

**Anchor:** You know how to process critique. You've improved before. You've pivoted and thrived. You've handled worse with less support.

**Transfer:** You decide to ask a question instead of defending. You stay open instead of bracing.

**Action:** You say, "That's fair. I hadn't seen it that way. What would have made it land better?"

That's mastery. Not because you controlled the other person, but because you regulated the conversation inside yourself *first*.

That's what inner STRATA work gives you: the ability to track your own signal and stop mistaking survival strategies for personality traits. Because here's the hard truth most people avoid: your default self-talk isn't neutral. It's inherited. It's rehearsed. It's conditioned from thousands of micro-moments where you didn't feel safe, seen, or enough. You can't overwrite that with affirmations. You have to recondition the system.

And that happens not in therapy, not in a journal, not on retreat, but in the three-second micro-choices of real life. That moment when you feel the urge to perform, or please, or prove—and you pause. You reroute. You choose a different lens.

The more you do this, the less your inner world becomes a courtroom and the more it becomes a command center. And from there, everything changes. You stop talking to yourself like a critic. You start talking like a strategist. You stop asking, "Am I good enough?" and start asking, "What would give me the best traction right now?" This isn't delusion. This is grounded, aware, real-time recalibration.

STRATA doesn't make you bulletproof. It makes you transparent, to yourself. And that self-transparency is what generates real presence. Because nothing is more magnetic than someone who isn't fighting their own reflection.

You've seen the opposite. The person whose entire energy is running a silent script—*Please approve of me. Please don't challenge me. Please validate me so I don't have to do it myself.* They don't even realize it, but their whole posture is compensation. Their conversation is technically fine, but it's built on a tremor. You can feel the self-doubt radiating off of them.

Now flip it. Think about someone who walks into a room not trying to perform, but simply *land*. They speak from alignment. Not because they're fearless, but because they're calibrated. Their inner conversation is rooted, so the external one has gravity. Even when they don't know something, they own it without flinching.

That's what STRATA helps you develop: not a script, but a spine. And that spine allows you say things you couldn't say before, not because the risk is gone, but because you know who's talking. You know when the voice in your head is your trained self, and when it's your twelve-year-old self. And that distinction lets you lead.

This work also changes how you recover, because sometimes, you *will* flinch. You *will* shrink. You *will* get reactive. STRATA doesn't make you perfect. But it does give you a map back to center.

You say the wrong thing in a meeting? Run the layers. You froze on stage? Run the layers. You lost your temper with your kid? Run the layers. Each time you do, you make the inner world a little safer to return to. And the safer it feels in there, the less you'll need to perform out here.

That's the paradox most people never realize: when you stop trying to be seen a certain way, you become more visible. Because your signal gets clean, and a clean signal is hard to ignore.

Let's talk about posture for a second. People assume body language is mostly about how you look. Open arms. Eye contact. Straight spine. But the most powerful posture shifts don't happen on the outside. They happen in your **emotional geometry**, your felt sense of position in the room.

Do you feel beneath them? Above them? Like a fraud? Like a threat? Like a kid? Like a ghost?

All of that is inner conversation. If you walk in believing you need to prove yourself, your body will tense, your tone will shift, and your listening will distort. You'll hear a neutral question as an attack. You'll over-explain. You'll rush to fill silence. But if you walk in knowing who you are, *not in theory, but in your system*, then your signal stays clean even under pressure.

STRATA trains this by repetition. Not by "positive thinking," but by repatterning your access point. You stop entering rooms with your father's voice in your head. You stop pitching with your last failure sitting on your chest. You stop showing up like the scared version of yourself who got passed over for the job ten years ago, and you start talking like someone who actually knows what they bring. Because you do. It just gets buried.

STRATA doesn't add something fake on top. It *unearths* the signal underneath the survival layer, and the fastest way to do that is to build the habit of asking:

## What conversation am I having with myself right now?

Not *what should I say?*

Not *what do they want to hear?*

But *what's my internal posture right now, and do I trust it to carry this moment?*

That question alone can reroute a lifetime of reaction because when the voice in your head stops being the enemy, it becomes the edge.

That's what STRATA gives you. Not a louder voice. A cleaner one. Not a tougher posture. A truer one. Not a mask of certainty. A lived clarity. So the next time the stakes rise, and they will, don't race to fix your words. Fix your **frame**.

Track your signal. Decode the trigger. Name the reframe. Return to the anchor. Transfer permission. Then take action. You won't just sound better. You'll *feel* real. And when you feel real, the room listens differently, because you're not just in the conversation. You *are* the conversation.

# CHAPTER 11

# WHEN THE ROOM IS ON FIRE

*"Things go wrong so that you appreciate them when they're right."*

— Rita Ora

*It was all going your way—*

*until it wasn't.*

*One offhand comment.*

*One glance you weren't supposed to catch.*

*And suddenly,*

*the ground tilted,*

*and you were fighting to stay in the room.*

## When the Room Is on Fire

There's a sound the room makes when things go sideways. It's not loud. It's not always verbal. But if you're tuned in, you hear it immediately—the subtle shift in tone, the drop in breath, the silence that isn't quiet so much as *braced*. Like the air just thickened and every word now carries more weight than it should. This is the crisis moment. And if you can't read it, you won't recover from it.

The change in the room is not just about what's said; it's about what's *felt*. When someone shuts down, when tempers flare, when the energy in the room moves from tension to threat, you've crossed a behavioral threshold. The people in front of you are no longer listening with curiosity. They're listening with armor. And if your strategy doesn't account for that shift, you'll escalate instead of de-escalate. You'll defend instead of reframe. You'll lose the room without even realizing it.

This is where most influence strategies collapse. They're optimized for neutral ground for meetings where everyone is calm, attentive, and open to persuasion. But STRATA was built differently. It was built to read live dynamics under pressure. It was designed to work when people aren't their best selves, when they're panicked, postured, angry, ashamed, or scared.

Crisis isn't just a context. It's a pressure test. And STRATA doesn't just help you speak well; it helps you *stay in the room* when everything starts to burn. So what does it look like to apply STRATA in moments of emotional volatility? Let's start where most people lose their footing: **triggers.**

When someone explodes in a meeting, or goes icy and cold, the instinct is to counter-punch or smooth it over. One person raises their voice, and you raise yours. Or worse, you try to pretend nothing just happened. But STRATA teaches us to track the **signal before the sound.** That means noticing the moment *before* the outburst: the shift in breath, the micro-expression of contempt, the flicker of disbelief when someone feels cornered.

People don't erupt out of nowhere. They signal. They brace. They test. And if you're fluent in STRATA, you learn to name what's happening without blame and that changes everything. Take a sales team leader who's just been told their strategy is "no longer competitive." You're facilitating a quarterly planning session, and you can feel the heat rise.

His face tightens. He interrupts. "We've hit our goals three quarters in a row. You want to talk competitive?"

Now the room is on edge. Most facilitators would panic. Backpedal. Deflect. Or try to "power through." But a STRATA practitioner does something different. You don't match the fire. You *anchor* to the heat. You slow your breath. You adjust your posture—no retreat, no advance. Just stillness. You hold eye contact not with defiance, but with grounded neutrality. And then you say: "I hear the pride in that—and the frustration. What I said clearly didn't land the way I meant it. Let me ask it a different way: where are we winning because of the current strategy, and where might we be surviving in spite of it?"

That's not a dodge. That's a reframe. And more importantly, it's a posture reset. You just acknowledged the heat, adjusted your signal, and reopened the conversation without collapsing your stance.

Crisis moments aren't just about resolution. They're about **holding shape**. Because once someone loses trust in your ability to stay with them through intensity, they stop hearing you altogether. You become just another voice trying to control the narrative. STRATA isn't about control. It's about calibration under pressure.

Let's take a more personal example. You're sitting across from your teenage daughter. She's failing a class, pulling away, and tonight she came home three hours past curfew. You've been worried. You've also been waiting for this conversation. But the moment you start talking, she rolls her eyes and says, "I knew this was coming. Can we *not* do this right now?"

Your blood pressure spikes. You're not just scared, you're offended. You want to lay down the law. Remind her of the rules. The disrespect. The risk. But STRATA teaches us that influence doesn't live in the "rules." It lives in the *read*.

So instead of punishing, you pause. You look at her, *really* look, and see the fatigue behind the defiance. The fear underneath the eye-roll. She's not dismissing you. She's bracing for another emotional blow.

So you anchor differently. "I know you're expecting a lecture. You probably deserve one, but that's not why I waited up. I'm here because I want to know what's happening underneath the surface, and I want you to know I can handle it—whatever it is."

She doesn't respond right away. But her shoulders soften. The air shifts. You just moved the conversation from confrontation to containment. That's STRATA in crisis: shifting the conversation from threat to tether.

When people are in pain, their communication isn't about logic. It's about *safety*. If they don't feel safe, they won't be honest. They'll either defend, detach, or disappear. And that's true in business, in parenting, in leadership, in marriage.

What STRATA gives you is a **map of posture under pressure**. It helps you see what others are bracing for before they ever say it. It gives you language for moments when language usually fails. And it gives you moves that don't just sound good, they *restore alignment* in real time.

Let's talk about team conflict. You're called in to mediate a breakdown between two department heads. One accuses the other of stealing credit. The other insists it was a team effort. The meetings have grown tense. Deadlines are missed, and HR is ready to escalate.

Most conflict resolution trainings would have you focus on listening skills, shared values, or finding common ground, but in STRATA, you're doing something deeper: **decoding the behavioral sequence** that led to rupture and guiding the team back to mutual permission.

That starts by **locating the signal conflict**, not just the surface issue. In this case, the credit issue isn't about recognition, it's about **trust** and **psychological threat**. One leader feels invisible. The other feels misunderstood. So instead of forcing a kumbaya conversation, you stage the room carefully. You seat them side by side, not across from each other. You open with posture, not policy. And you say: "We're not here to solve everything today. We're here to understand how we got here. Because until we can name the breakdown clearly, every solution will feel like a patch."

Then you observe. You track whose body tightens when blame comes up. Who jumps in to defend before listening. Who goes quiet when truth gets too close. These are all **access points**, and STRATA teaches you to use them, not to call people out, but to draw them in. You might say: "I'm noticing every time we mention 'team effort,' one of you leans back and the other looks down. That tells me the words don't feel safe yet. Can we pause there?"

That moment—just that pause—can reset an entire trajectory. Now you're not talking about behavior *in theory*. You're tracking behavior *in real time*, and when people feel seen in that way, not judged, but witnessed, they start to soften. Not always. Not instantly. But often enough that the room begins to breathe again.

This is the silent genius of STRATA: it doesn't demand a better version of people. It meets them in the version they're already showing and works from there. Most frameworks try to "fix" behavior. STRATA reads it. This means you don't waste time telling people how they *should* be responding. You use their current posture, tone, rhythm, and resistance as the actual material for reconnection.

Take a hospital team in crisis. A critical medication error occurred on the night shift, and no one is taking responsibility. The medical director is livid. The nursing supervisor is defensive. A young resident is visibly shaken. The air is tight. Legal is involved. In most systems, this turns into an investigation. Fingers point. Blame gets passed down the chain. But in STRATA, your goal is not blame, it's *alignment under pressure*. That means restoring signal clarity first.

So you start not by asking *what happened*, but *what got missed*. You say: "Before we map the timeline, I want to ask: when did the room first feel off? When did we feel something wasn't right, even if we didn't have the facts yet?"

This does two things. First, it invites reflection instead of defense. Second, it brings people back to signal, how they *knew* something was wrong *before* they could prove it. You're training the team to trust their behavioral radar again. And that's a critical reframe. Because in crisis, most people lose faith in their instincts. STRATA reactivates it by saying: you *felt* it. Now let's name it, and let's move from that place forward.

Let's shift to a personal crisis, one where you're not the facilitator, but the one in the heat. Imagine you're the CEO of a startup. Your funding just fell through. Your team doesn't know yet. Payroll is due next week. You're supposed to be leading a town hall to roll out your Q4 roadmap, and you're unraveling inside.

Here's where STRATA turns inward. Before you walk into that room, you pause, not to plan your talking points, but to calibrate your *own* signal. What are you broadcasting? Desperation? False confidence? Resentment? You can't fake posture, not for long. But you *can* ground it. So you slow down. You breathe into your belly. You speak your fear out loud, to yourself, or to someone safe. You say: "I'm terrified of what this will do to my team. But I know if I hide that fear, it'll leak. And if it leaks, I lose them."

Then you walk into the room. Not with a mask, but with **measured clarity**. You start with: "There's no easy way to say this. But I want to say it to your faces, not your inboxes." You name the crisis. You name the impact. And you name the commitment to transparency, not spin. That's STRATA at its core: behavioral honesty in high-stakes moments.

This chapter is about emotional precision, not performative courage. It's about how to *stay real* without unraveling. Because people don't need you to be perfect in conflict, they need you to be *present*. They need to see that you can feel the pressure and still hold the room without flinching or fleeing.

One of the most powerful moments in STRATA happens when someone *names the thing everyone is avoiding*, not to shame but to settle. Like the client who finally says, "I can tell you're not sold, and I'd rather pause here and talk honestly than keep pushing a pitch that doesn't land." Or the partner who says, "We keep fighting about logistics, but I don't think that's the real issue. I think we've both been scared to say we feel distant."

Those aren't rehearsed lines. They're real reads. They come from tracking signal in real time and having the courage to *say the thing* without accusation, without agenda, but with undeniable clarity. Let's not pretend this is easy. Conflict is disorienting. Crisis is heavy. The body tightens, the mind races, and instinct tells you to fix or flee. But STRATA offers a third move: *feel, then frame*. You feel the shift. You name it without panic. You frame it so people can re-enter the room with you.

This is why STRATA isn't just a method for conversation. It's a method for *restoration*. It gives you the tools to repair what feels broken, not through slogans or structure, but through behavioral fluency.

When conflict is sharp, you don't need volume, you need signal clarity. When crisis hits, you don't need answers, you need anchored presence. And when the room is on fire, you don't lead with persuasion, you lead with *perception*.

The room wants to know: can you see us? Can you *feel* what just happened? Can you name the thing we're too scared to name? That's not emotional intelligence. That's emotional leadership. And STRATA makes it teachable. It's not some mystical charisma. It's calibration. It's practice. It's the repeated act of tracking where the energy actually is, not where you wish it was, and learning to speak from there. Because here's the truth: Conflict is never just about content. It's about *posture collision*. And crisis isn't just an interruption. It's a window into what the system was always wired to do under stress.

STRATA teaches you to listen at that level, so when the room breaks, you don't. You bend. You track. You hold. And from there, you lead.

# CHAPTER 12

# STRATA ARCHETYPES

*"History doesn't repeat itself, but it often rhymes."*

— Mark Twain

*You'd never met them before.*

*But within minutes,*

*you knew exactly how this would go.*

*The words were different.*

*The posture was not.*

*You weren't reading the person—*

*you were reading the pattern.*

## STRATA Archetypes

Some people don't need a script to throw off your entire conversation, they *are* the disruption. You know the ones. The moment they enter the room, it tilts. The vibe shifts. The rhythm disappears, and suddenly, the STRATA techniques that worked perfectly in the last meeting fall flat. Why?

Because misalignment doesn't always come from the message, it comes from the *person*. The way they interpret tone. The way they posture in silence. The way their nervous system reacts to pressure. Some people aren't reacting to *you*, they're reacting to the *frame* of the conversation itself. And if you don't recognize that early, you waste time recalibrating to someone who's playing a different game entirely. This is where the STRATA Archetypes come in.

STRATA Archetypes are not personality types, they're behavioral *modes*—patterns people default to when they feel threatened, disoriented, or emotionally invested but disconnected. These archetypes show up most in moments that matter: when you're closing a deal, having a hard conversation, leading a team, pitching an idea, or challenging someone's worldview. And unless you know how to spot them, you'll try to sell clarity to someone seeking control, or offer solutions to someone secretly performing.

This chapter isn't about diagnosing people, it's about decoding patterns. When you recognize the archetype in front of you, you stop reacting to their behavior. You start responding to the *signal beneath it*.

Let's begin with one of the most common, and misunderstood archetypes: **The Performer.**

The Performer looks like they're on your side. They nod. They smile. They even compliment your pitch. But underneath it all, there's a subtle dissonance. Something feels… off. You finish a powerful point, and instead of letting it land, they jump in with a story of their own. They agree with everything and commit to nothing. They dominate airtime but avoid decisions. And when it comes time to move the conversation forward, they disappear into generalities or defer to someone else. What's going on?

The Performer is chasing **status over signal.** Their behavior is calibrated to keep control of the spotlight, not necessarily to solve a problem or reach alignment. They need to be seen as insightful, helpful, or high-status, which means they often "yes-and" you while subtly pulling the focus back to themselves.

If you're not careful, you'll mistake enthusiasm for buy-in. You'll think the Performer is a warm lead, a collaborative partner, or a supportive stakeholder, until you realize they haven't actually taken a position. STRATA teaches you to stop measuring engagement by volume and start measuring it by *posture*. The Performer often leans in with words, but leans out with presence.

The STRATA move? Don't interrupt their rhythm, but don't orbit around them either. A subtle reframing technique is key here: instead of responding to their stories or affirmations, you ask for **ownership**. "So what would that look like if we committed to it on your side?"

That simple question reveals whether the Performer is actually in alignment or just auditioning for a role in the room.

Next up: **The Ghoster.**

This archetype may seem quiet at first, but the damage they do isn't in the moment, it's after the call ends. After the meeting concludes. After the deck is sent. You felt like it went well. They nodded. They said all the right things. They even sounded excited. And then… nothing. No reply. No feedback. No follow-up. Just silence.

The Ghoster thrives on **avoidance masked as politeness**. They don't want conflict. They don't want to say no. They don't even want to admit they're unsure. So instead, they disappear, letting time do what they weren't willing to do directly.

This is brutal in sales, leadership, and relationships alike. Ghosters aren't malicious, they're *self-protective*. Their nervous system interprets clarity as confrontation, so they play it safe until they're far enough away to say nothing at all.

STRATA teaches you not to chase Ghosters but to *collapse ambiguity before it begins*. When you sense the soft nods, the delayed language, the "This sounds really interesting" with no follow-up questions, don't interpret that as a green light. Instead, add a small, disarming reframe: "Before we close out, I want to ask something I don't always ask. On a scale from 'I'm totally aligned' to 'I'm not sure I'd ever follow through on this,' where are you actually sitting right now, no judgment either way?"

That kind of permission-based clarity shakes the Ghoster out of their pattern without pressure, but with posture. And if they still vanish? That's feedback too. Don't take it personally; just move forward without dragging their silence into your confidence.

Now let's talk about **The Debater.**

You know them the moment they start talking. Everything is a test. They interrupt mid-sentence. They poke holes. They ask you to prove it, then question your data when you do. It's not always hostile. Sometimes it's playful, sometimes it's inquisitive. But it always leaves you slightly off balance, like you're in court instead of a conversation.

The Debater isn't always trying to win, they're trying to *regain control of the emotional landscape.* They've likely been burned before. Or they pride themselves on skepticism. Or they just feel safer when they're steering the intellectual tone of the exchange. Either way, what they're really saying is: "I'll connect with you if you can hold your ground without flinching."

And that's your STRATA signal. You don't meet the Debater with more data. You meet them with **neutral gravity.** "You're right to ask that. A lot of smart people push back on that point. What usually opens things up is this…"

Notice the shift? You didn't concede. You didn't challenge. You *anchored.* Debaters relax when they feel you're not afraid of tension. If they keep escalating, you can even trigger a gentle transfer: "Let me flip it. If this were your challenge to solve, where would you start?" Now they're co-owning the frame instead of testing yours.

Next: **The Pleaser.**

This is the person who agrees too quickly. Nods constantly. Echoes your phrasing. They seem easy to work with, open-minded, gracious. But after a while, you notice something unsettling: they're not actually moving forward. They're absorbing everything you say, but offering little in return. They praise your pitch but won't take a position. You leave the meeting feeling affirmed, but strangely hollow.

That's the Pleaser's pattern. It's not deception. It's defense. Pleasers are often wired to smooth tension before it forms. Whether it's from family dynamics, workplace politics, or cultural expectations, they've learned that the way to stay safe in a room is to stay likable. That means minimizing disagreement, staying upbeat, and keeping others comfortable even if they have no intention of following through.

But STRATA doesn't reward harmony. It rewards honesty. So the move here is to interrupt the feedback loop not with confrontation, but with *choice*. Try this: "I'm getting the sense that you're being really open here, which I appreciate. But I also want to make sure this is actually helpful to you. Would it be more useful if I pulled back, or would you want to go deeper?"

You've just given the Pleaser an off-ramp. And more often than not, they'll either open up or opt out. Either way, you've moved from polite noise to real signal.

The other STRATA move with a Pleaser is to watch how they react when someone else disagrees. If they suddenly shift tone or echo the stronger personality, you've found the real gravity of the room. And now you know who to read next.

Then there's **The Stonewaller.**

This one's harder to pin down. They're present, but unmovable. No facial expression. No questions. No feedback. You try to calibrate to them, but they give you nothing. You can feel them holding back, but you can't tell whether it's disinterest, judgment, or just detachment.

Stonewallers don't always mean "no." Sometimes, they mean "not yet." But when you mistake their silence for rejection, you over-adjust.

You start rushing, over-explaining, filling the gaps. And that only reinforces their resistance.

Here's what STRATA teaches you: *Silence is not absence. It's data.* The key with a Stonewaller is pacing. You don't mirror their distance. You hold your own posture and invite, not demand, participation. You might say: "You seem like someone who doesn't give their attention lightly. Totally fair. If I'm off the mark, I'll stop. But if something's landing, I'd rather build from there."

You're not trying to melt the wall. You're respecting it while signaling strength. That subtle reframe changes everything. The Stonewaller may not become warm, but they will start listening. And when they do engage, it'll be real.

Also: pay attention to what *they* respond to. Do their eyes shift when you speak about risk? Do they glance at a colleague when budget is mentioned? Those micro-reactions are your leverage points. With a Stonewaller, it's less about what they say and more about what they *can't fully suppress.*

Now we hit **The Steamroller.**

This archetype is unmistakable. They interrupt. Dominate. Reframe everything to be about them. If you're presenting, they hijack. If you're facilitating, they argue. They don't mean to ruin the room, but they do. Because they confuse dominance with leadership. And they're used to others folding.

Here's the trap: trying to out-assert them. If you escalate, they double down. If you withdraw, they take over, so STRATA offers a third path: *anchored redirection.*

First, recognize what they're signaling. Most Steamrollers aren't trying to sabotage, they're trying to be heard, but their nervous system only knows volume and velocity. So give them presence without surrendering control. "I can tell this matters to you and you've clearly thought about it. I want to make sure we get to that. Let me park that thread for a second while I land this piece, and then we'll circle back."

You're not ignoring them. You're containing them. And once they know you're not afraid of their energy, they often calm down. Because what Steamrollers truly need isn't obedience, it's *a frame stronger than theirs*.

Bonus tip: if the Steamroller is a high-status individual (a CEO, a founder, a team lead), redirecting them respectfully becomes even more powerful. It signals not just command but *equality*. And that's a rare experience for them.

Finally, let's talk about a special archetype: **The STRATA Technician.**

This one's closer to home. Because sometimes... it's *you*. This is the person who's read the book. Studied the moves. Practiced the techniques. But now they're stuck *inside* the model. They're running STRATA like a checklist. They're hyper-aware of posture, rhythm, resistance and because of that, they lose the moment itself. They sound polished but not present. Precise but not human. Their signal doesn't feel *felt*, it feels *calculated*.

This happens when someone turns STRATA into *performance* instead of *presence*. It's not wrong. It's just early. Mastery isn't about memorizing the moves, it's about internalizing the rhythm. Knowing when to bend the rule. When to leave space. When to follow the tension instead of managing it.

If you ever find yourself becoming the Technician—overanalyzing, scripting reactions, trying to "STRATA" your way through intimacy— pause. Breathe. Ask yourself: "What's happening right now that isn't in my notes?"

That's your return to the room. Because STRATA was never meant to make you robotic, it was meant to make you *free* to move through any room, any rupture, any resistance, with presence that holds.

So what do you do with all of this?

You don't label people forever. You don't assume fixed types. You *recognize patterns in motion* and then adjust your STRATA moves to meet them. You stop treating misalignment as a problem and start treating it as a roadmap. When someone "goes Performer" or "starts Ghosting" or "Debates every word," they're not trying to ruin your influence. They're trying to protect something. Maybe it's reputation. Maybe it's safety. Maybe it's certainty.

Your job isn't to fix them. It's to read them. To know which room you're in *before* the conversation starts collapsing. To stop pushing, and start aligning. STRATA doesn't just work in the ideal moments. It works in the friction.

And these archetypes? They're not obstacles. They're signals. The more fluently you read them, the less likely you are to lose the room. Even when the room is trying to lose you first.

# CHAPTER 13

# CALIBRATION

*"Adaptability is about the powerful difference between adapting to cope and adapting to win."*

— Max McKeown

*The shift hit hard.*

*Tone. Tempo. Target.*

*One wrong move,*

*and you were done.*

*So you read it.*

*You pivoted.*

*And in the space of a breath—*

*you turned the ambush into the advantage.*

## Calibration

Now that you understand STRATA, you might be tempted to treat it like a playbook. A sequence of steps. A toolkit you can pull from when the room feels tense, or the pitch feels stale, or your buyer is stone-faced and quiet. That's not wrong, but it's incomplete. STRATA isn't just a way to diagnose or dissect a conversation, it's a way to *be* in a conversation. And that means knowing not just *what* to use, but *when*, *why*, and *how* to shift in the moment. That ability? It's called calibration.

Calibration is what separates someone who knows STRATA from someone who can lead with it in real time. It's not just what you say or which layer you apply, it's the **timing, tone, and tempo** of the move. It's the difference between a jazz musician and a piano student. Both might play the same notes, but one can feel the rhythm shift before it even happens and adjust mid-measure without blinking. That's what this chapter is about: learning to feel the room, respond in real time, and adjust your presence without losing your footing.

Let me tell you about Jamie. Jamie was one of the most technically skilled salespeople I'd ever worked with. He was sharp, articulate, and incredibly prepared. He could map out conversations in advance, anticipate objections, and build beautiful value stories. On paper, Jamie was a STRATA success story waiting to happen. But when it came time to execute in the real world, when deals slowed or meetings got awkward, Jamie would freeze. Or worse, he'd try to fix everything with more words. More explanations. More urgency. And the more he did, the less the room responded.

What Jamie lacked wasn't insight. It was calibration. He could name the STRATA layers intellectually, but he hadn't learned to *feel* them. He hadn't built the muscle to notice the subtle cues that signaled a shift was needed: a client crossing their arms, a moment of dead silence, a smile that didn't reach the eyes. These weren't big red flags. They were small, behavioral tells. And he missed them, not because he didn't care, but because he was locked in his own plan.

That's what most of us do. We cling to what we *planned* to say, instead of responding to what's actually happening. We prioritize performance over presence. And that creates the exact gap STRATA was built to close. Calibration isn't about having perfect awareness.

It's about noticing the tension, naming the mismatch, and adjusting without collapsing your signal.

Here's what that looks like. Let's say you're in a pitch meeting. You've just made a bold claim, a provocative insight that reframes the buyer's current approach. You're confident in your point, and it's rooted in research. But the buyer suddenly stiffens. Their rhythm slows. They stop making eye contact. You sense friction. Most people, in that moment, either double down ("Let me explain further!") or backpedal ("Of course, that might not apply to you..."). Both are common. Neither are calibrated.

The calibrated move? You pause. You read the room. You notice what *their* body is doing, what *your* body is doing, and you ask: Did I trigger something that needs space to land? Is this resistance, or just processing? Do I need to reinforce Signal or shift into a softer Reframe? Calibration means making those micro-decisions without performing them out loud. It means letting silence work for you instead of panicking to fill it.

One of the most misunderstood aspects of calibration is timing. People often ask, "How do I know *when* to move to the next layer?" And the answer is maddeningly simple: *You feel it.* Not in some mystical, guru-like way, but in a grounded, embodied way. When you're present, when your attention is on the *room* instead of your *script*, you begin to sense when energy shifts. You feel when something has landed and when it hasn't. You know when the posture has softened, when urgency is rising, or when your own tone has drifted too far off center.

And when you feel it, you don't overcorrect. That's the trap. Most people sense something is off and immediately try to *fix* it. They explain more. They pivot too hard. They change the subject, hoping to regain control. But calibration isn't about control, it's about alignment. It's the gentle nudge, not the sledgehammer. It's the shift in rhythm, not the change in genre.

Let me give you another example. I once worked with a VP of Strategy at a biotech firm. We'll call her Lauren. She had a habit of shutting down when challenged. She didn't yell. She didn't withdraw. She went flat. Neutral. Her voice would lower, her eye contact would vanish, and her responses would become strictly informational. This pattern caused huge issues with her team, who interpreted it as coldness or disengagement.

When we began working together using STRATA, it became clear that her flattening wasn't about disinterest. It was her version of **self-calming**; her way of staying composed under pressure. But here's the thing: even though *she* thought she was being neutral, her team was reading it as rejection.

Calibration, for Lauren, meant two things. First, she had to recognize that her internal state wasn't matching her external signal. Second, she had to build the skill of subtly adjusting her posture and tone to reflect presence. even when she felt unsure inside. That didn't mean pretending. It meant staying aligned. When she learned to soften her posture, lift her gaze, and use a slightly warmer tone, her feedback conversations transformed. Same content. New signal. Better outcomes. That's the power of calibration.

But this chapter wouldn't be complete without talking about the internal calibration—the part most people miss. Because yes, STRATA is about reading others, but it's also about reading *yourself* in the moment. Your own tells. Your own patterns. Your own nervous system.

Have you ever felt your heart rate spike in a conversation and suddenly lost track of what you were saying? Or had an internal voice whisper, "This isn't working," and then felt your energy drop? That's not just anxiety. That's data. Your nervous system is flagging something. Calibration teaches you to listen to those signals, not as fears to override, but as insights to integrate.

In my own career, I've had moments where I could feel a conversation slipping away, not because the other person said anything definitive, but because *I* lost presence. I started watching their face too closely, hunting for approval. I rushed my words. I broke eye contact. And every time, it was because something in me got triggered, some old story about needing to prove myself. When I learned to recognize that internal shift, I stopped chasing control and started reclaiming center.

Calibration doesn't mean perfection. It means responsiveness. It means staying awake to what's happening *in you* and *around you* so you can make cleaner choices. And yes, this takes practice.

You build calibration the way you build fluency in a language: through exposure, repetition, and reflection. You run scenarios. You study body language. You record yourself and watch for shifts. You debrief after meetings and ask, "Where did I feel tight? Where did I feel flow? What signals did I miss?"

Over time, your system gets faster. You stop relying on mental checklists. Your body becomes the instrument. And you start leading conversations with a kind of grounded flexibility, firm in your message, fluid in your delivery.

When I teach STRATA in workshops, I often use the metaphor of sailing. Anyone can steer a boat in calm waters. But real sailors calibrate constantly. They adjust to wind shifts. They scan the horizon. They feel the rudder with their hands and the sail tension in their fingertips. They don't wait for the storm, they read the sky. STRATA is the same. The better you calibrate, the less you're surprised. And the fewer dramatic pivots you need to make.

So how do you know when you're calibrated? You're not rattled by silence. You're not chasing permission. You're not trapped in performance. You're reading the room like a second language and speaking to what's actually there, not what you hoped would be. You're not just delivering STRATA. You're embodying it.

What separates mastery from competence in calibration isn't just what you notice in others, it's what you learn to notice in yourself. The truth is, most miscalibrations don't start with the other person. They start with your own signal slipping.

You might be projecting urgency when none is needed, not because the room calls for it, but because your own internal tension is rising. You might over-anchor not because the moment is right, but because you're trying to lock down something before it drifts out of your control. These moves don't happen because you're manipulative or bad at this. They happen because underneath the professional posture, there's a very human system trying to stay safe, seen, and in charge.

And that's the deeper layer of calibration—what I call *emotional fidelity*. It's not just about whether your move matches the moment; it's about whether your move is *honest* to the deeper intention beneath it.

Here's what I mean. I once worked with a leader who had incredible tactical skill. Let's call her Vanessa. She knew how to run a room, command attention, and shift gears on a dime. But in moments of high stakes—when investors pushed back, or a direct report disappointed her—her calibration would vanish. She'd go icy, flat. Almost robotic. Like someone had flipped a switch and drained the life from her voice. At first glance, it looked like executive control. But it wasn't. It was retreat.

After some deeper coaching, we uncovered the root: Vanessa had grown up in a household where being emotional, especially angry or uncertain, meant being punished or ignored. Her adult-self had learned to suppress any signal of inner instability by going stoic. But in a leadership role, that habit wasn't serving her. It wasn't keeping her in control, it was making her unreadable. And unreadable leaders don't inspire trust.

Calibration, for her, wasn't about learning new tactics. It was about building the internal permission to stay human in the moment. To let a flicker of disappointment show. To let curiosity replace critique. To be seen adjusting, not collapsing. And that's the paradox of true calibration: the more refined it becomes, the less performance is required. The closer you get to honest presence, the less energy it takes to influence well.

So how do you cultivate that? You build the reps where they matter most on the inside. Start with reflection after the moment, not just what happened, but *what you were feeling*.

Ask:

- Where did I go flat, or fake?
- What made me feel like I had to push?
- Was I trying to win, protect, or perform?

This internal map becomes your calibration blueprint, because when you know your default patterns under pressure, you can begin to catch them as they rise and choose something different. You'll notice the speed creeping into your voice and say, "Ah—there it is. My need to convince." And you'll breathe. Soften. Wait.

You'll feel the old tension in your chest that says, "They're not listening," and instead of powering through, you'll drop your shoulders and check in: "Hey, before we go further, is this actually landing?"

These aren't tactics. They're trust behaviors. And trust, whether in leadership, sales, or relationships, is built not from perfection, but from your ability to adapt transparently. People don't trust the person who always has the right answer. They trust the person who can *see* when something shifted, name it, and stay grounded in the process.

Let me give you a personal example. Years ago, I was invited to run a half-day training with a team that was completely burned out. They weren't interested in new models. They didn't want motivation, they wanted space. But no one had said that out loud.

I opened with STRATA, thinking I'd ease them in. Ten minutes in, I felt the room go stale. No one pushed back, but no one was leaning in either. I could feel the disconnect, like fog creeping across the floor.

Old me might've doubled down. Told more stories. Switched frameworks. Tried harder. Instead, I stopped. I said, "You don't need another model, do you?"

They blinked. One woman nodded slowly.

"What do you need?" I asked.

Someone finally said, "We need someone to actually ask us how we're doing, not just teach us how to perform better."

That moment turned the day. We didn't do the curriculum. We talked about burnout. About expectations. About the pressure to always be "on" even when you're depleted. And you know what happened? By the end of the session, *then* they wanted to learn STRATA. Because they finally felt seen.

That's calibration. Not as a technique, but as an act of presence. And it only happens when you stop trying to protect your plan and start listening to what the room is actually asking for.

Let's bring this home with a final note about ownership.

Calibration isn't just the hidden skill of great communicators. It's the glue that keeps your identity aligned with your influence. It's the muscle that lets you pivot without panic. It's the mechanism that turns strategy into leadership and leadership into trust.

Anyone can deliver a rehearsed pitch. Anyone can memorize the layers of STRATA. But only someone calibrated can *respond* in real time when the energy shifts, the buy-in stalls, or the resistance surfaces in a way you didn't expect. And make no mistake—it will.

There is no path where STRATA goes exactly how you imagined. There is no sequence of events where everything unfolds on your timeline, with clean signals and perfect responses. That's fantasy.

But what's real—what's powerful—is the *capacity* you build when you train for flexibility, attunement, and nuance. When you stop clinging to control and instead commit to *leading the moment as it is, not as you wish it were.*

That's when you stop pitching and start partnering. That's when you stop talking to personas and start speaking to people. That's when

STRATA stops being a model and becomes the way you move. And all of that? It starts with calibration.

# BONUS CHAPTER

# THE GUARANTEED SALE THAT WAS LOST

This chapter wasn't part of the plan.

By the time I wrote this, the manuscript was already finished, edited, and practically out the door. But something happened on vacation that I couldn't ignore. It was one of those rare moments where the theory you teach every day walks right up to you and dares you to prove it works.

This wasn't a client meeting. It wasn't research. It was supposed to be rest—just me and my wife, disconnected from everything. But what unfolded was such a clear demonstration of what happens *when you don't use STRATA* that I couldn't leave it out.

It became an accidental experiment that showed me, in real time, how a guaranteed sale can implode, not from price, not from product, but from blindness.

## The Setup

If you've ever owned a timeshare, you know the drill: the so-called "account review." They tell you it'll take an hour, just a quick check-in to confirm your details. In reality, it's a sales pitch dressed as customer care. They dangle a gift card or discount to get you in the seat, then aim to upsell you into a higher membership tier.

My wife and I knew exactly what it was. And here's the key: *we were ready to buy.*

We'd already talked about upgrading before the trip. We knew the numbers. We knew the benefits. We were set on moving into a higher tier that cost significantly more but came with the perks we wanted.

This wasn't a "maybe." It wasn't a "convince me." It was a done deal. We walked into that room ready to spend. All the rep had to do was tell us where to sign. All he had to do was *not mess it up.*

## The Experiment

I train people to read human behavior for a living. So sometimes, when the moment feels right, I run what I call "live experiments." This was one of those times.

When the rep approached, his energy hit like a spotlight. He had a big smile, high enthusiasm, and rapid-fire rapport. For most buyers, that energy might land well. But for me, it was the perfect chance to test his adaptability.

So I deliberately did the opposite. I sat back. crossed my arms, turned my knees slightly away, and gave clipped, one-word answers. My tone went flat. My posture said *closed.* In STRATA terms, I was broadcasting *Signal failure*—loudly. This was the moment to see if he could read it.

## Signal Failure

If he'd noticed what STRATA teaches, he would've seen it instantly: My posture signaled distance. My tone signaled detachment. My lack of engagement signaled disconnection.

The correct move? Match the buyer's energy. Slow down. Drop the tone. Rebuild comfort. Re-sync the pace. But instead, he pushed harder. His voice stayed bright and animated, completely misaligned with the energy across the table. The more he talked, the more obvious it became that he wasn't reading *me*. He was following *script*.

He didn't see the crossed arms. He didn't hear the flat tone. He didn't feel the stillness in the room. In STRATA terms, he failed the first layer. He ignored the *Signal*.

## Trigger Breakdown

Then came the subtle pivot. Midway through his presentation, he said something that genuinely caught my attention. It was a brief mention about a program perk that solved a real problem we'd had in the past.

That was my internal trigger. I leaned forward slightly. My hands opened. I made eye contact. My tone shifted. It was an unmistakable signal of re-engagement, *a window opening*.

And yet... nothing. He didn't pause. He didn't adjust. He didn't seize the moment. Instead, he steamrolled right through the opening. That's the tragedy of not recognizing a *Trigger*. He hit one; he just didn't know it. Had he noticed, he could've said, "You leaned in there. Sounds like that part resonated. Tell me more about what stood out."

That one sentence could have reconnected us completely. Instead, he lost me again.

## Reframe Collapse

As he went deeper into the pitch, something else became painfully clear: everything he said was framed around *him*. He told stories about his experience, his excitement for the product, what *he* loved most about the upgrade. Every example, every anecdote was told through his lens, not mine. He didn't reframe anything into my world. He didn't translate features into outcomes that mattered to *us*.

In STRATA, this is where real influence happens or dies. Reframing isn't about changing the topic; it's about changing the lens. He could've said: "You mentioned you travel often during the off-season. Here's how this upgrade actually saves you money during those months."

Instead, he stayed locked in *his* frame. By the time he finished, we weren't just unpersuaded, we were emotionally unplugged. The conversation was about *him*, and we were guests in it.

## Anchor Loss

Halfway through, the rep excused himself and returned with a "sales director." And that was the moment the anchor broke. Bringing in the director wasn't just unnecessary, it was disastrous.

It told me he'd lost control. It told me the company didn't trust him to close. And when the director sat down, it only got worse. The director launched into a long, meandering story about *his* career, how he'd started in sales, worked his way up, built a team. None of it connected to our situation. It wasn't relevant, it wasn't relational, and it sure as hell wasn't helpful. It was pure ego.

It re-anchored the entire dynamic. At the start of that meeting, my anchor was *I'm going to buy big today*. By the midpoint, it shifted to *I just want to leave*. He didn't realize it, but his lack of awareness had re-anchored my intent downward. And the director's intrusion sealed it.

What had started as a guaranteed sale became a slow leak of credibility. Every signal missed pushed the anchor lower, until "upgrade" turned into "just buy something small and get out."

## Transfer Failure

Eventually, we did buy something, but not what we came for. We purchased a small points package a bare minimum. Enough to justify the time we'd spent, but a fraction of what we'd intended to buy.

That's not a "win." It's a *misfire*. Because here's the truth: the rep *did* transfer me, but to the wrong action. He didn't transfer me toward excitement, confidence, or expansion. He transferred me toward retreat. That's the hidden danger in blind selling. When you can't read the room, you're still transferring emotion—you're just transferring the wrong one.

## Action (and the Cost)

When the deal closed, he probably celebrated. A sale's a sale, right? Except it wasn't. He had no idea he'd just walked away from a 10x opportunity. He didn't lose the sale; he lost *the scale* of it. He never realized he'd reprogrammed the buyer's psychology downward.

That's what poor presence costs. Not zeroes and ones. *Multiples*. If he'd used STRATA. If he'd paused to read the *Signal*, adjusted to the *Trigger*, reframed into *my world*, re-anchored to the original intent, and transferred cleanly, he would've closed the tier we walked in ready to buy. Instead, he used enthusiasm as a shield and left most of our money on the table.

## The Industry Lens

Now, zoom out. This isn't just about one rep. This is systemic. The timeshare industry boasts a 10–20% close rate on average. The "elite" reps barely touch 30%. That means 7 out of 10 people walk away without buying even though they're offered perks just to show up.

And here's the kicker: many of those lost buyers *wanted* to buy, just like we did. They weren't priced out. They were *misread out*. That's why STRATA exists. Because scripts, charisma, and canned objections can't read a room. Only presence can. And presence can't be faked, but it can be learned.

## Rewriting the Scene: What Should Have Happened

If we rewound that conversation and ran it through STRATA, here's how it would have unfolded:

- **Signal:** He sees the closed posture, the low tone, the turned knees and matches energy. He slows down, gets grounded, and meets me where I am.
- **Trigger:** He notices when I lean in and asks the right question: *"What caught your attention just now?"*
- **Reframe:** He connects the upgrade to my life, not his life and his script. He translates benefits into my world.
- **Anchor:** He keeps the focus on the purchase we came in ready to make reinforcing, not diminishing, the intent.
- **Transfer:** He ends the meeting by reinforcing confidence, clarity, and ownership of the decision.
- **Action:** We walk out buying at the higher tier not because we were sold, but because we were *seen.*

That's what STRATA does. It doesn't teach manipulation. It teaches *alignment.*

## Why This Story Matters

I didn't write this chapter to embarrass that rep. He wasn't bad. He was doing what he'd been taught. That's the real problem. The industry trained him to be blind, and he thought he was doing everything right. He smiled big. He stayed energetic. He followed the script. He powered through objections that weren't even there. And in doing so, he lost a sale that was already his.

The painful irony? I wanted to buy. He didn't lose me to logic; he lost me to *misalignment*. That's the hidden cost of ignoring human signals. The rep's company will record it as a sale. The spreadsheets will show success.

But the real story? They left thousands on the table and the buyer walked away less connected than when he walked in. That's what STRATA prevents. It keeps guaranteed wins from turning into accidental losses.

## Final Reflection

That day, I realized something I've seen in every industry, every profession, every human exchange: Opportunity doesn't vanish. It gets *transferred away*.

When you misread a signal, ignore a trigger, frame it in your own world, lose the anchor, and transfer the wrong emotion, you don't just fail to persuade. You convince the other person to retreat.

Presence is precision. Influence is timing. And STRATA is the structure that keeps you from losing what was already yours. The room was open. The buyer was ready. The deal was waiting.

He didn't lose the sale because I said no. He lost it because he never saw yes.

# EPILOGUE

# THE MOMENT THAT CHANGES EVERYTHING

Every strategy eventually meets a mirror. And that mirror is you.

All the tools, techniques, and behavioral blueprints in STRATA were never meant to stay on the page. The information in this book wasn't designed to impress, it was designed to equip. To prepare you for the moment when theory becomes reality, when preparation meets pressure, and when your words either land or they don't.

STRATA isn't about creating a persona. It's about aligning with your real power and then using it to move people, moments, and markets. If you've made it this far, you've absorbed a language that goes beyond conversation. You've stepped into a deeper understanding of perception, protection, and permission.

But before we close this book, we have to come full circle. Because influence—real influence—isn't something you do to others. It's something you *become*.

Let's revisit the journey.

In **Signal,** you learned how to see past the surface. To read urgency, rhythm, posture, tone, and presence—not just as traits, but as tells. You discovered how to see people not for what they say, but for where they are in that moment.

**Trigger** pulled back the veil. You stopped accepting resistance at face value and started recognizing it for what it really is—protection. A sign that something's at stake. You learned to name the deeper need behind the pushback.

**Reframe** showed you how to shift perspective. Not with argument, but with precision. You didn't have to overpower the current narrative, you just had to reveal the one they hadn't yet considered.

**Anchor** made the insight stick. You saw how emotion seals belief, how ownership cements it, and how context protects it. You learned to embed the message in a way that made it *feel* true, not just sound true.

**Transfer** passed the baton. You realized that people don't just want answers, they want to recognize themselves in the solution. When they can see their own fingerprints on the idea, they don't just accept it, they fight for it.

And finally, **Action**. The moment where belief becomes behavior. Where posture turns into movement, because it's not real until they act.

But now we arrive at the part that's most often skipped in frameworks like this: what it all means for *you*.

STRATA wasn't just about giving you tools to lead others. It was always about calling you into your own leadership. So here's the real question: Where in your life are you still waiting for permission? Where are you hoping someone else will make the first move, validate your presence, or open the door?

That's the paradox of influence. The people who learn to read everyone else—the empaths, the high EQ performers, the ones who notice everything—are often the last to advocate for themselves.

Why? Because they're used to making space for others. But STRATA doesn't just ask you to *read* the room, it asks you to *own* your place in it. And that starts by flipping your own frame.

I'll tell you a story. One that didn't make it into any keynote, but it shaped everything I teach. Years ago, I was standing in a hotel hallway waiting to go on stage. It was one of those big corporate gigs, a big client, big stakes, a big room. I'd done my prep. I knew my material. But I couldn't shake the voice in my head saying, "They're going to see through you."

The voice wasn't loud. It was subtle. That's how self-doubt often works. It doesn't yell; it whispers. And in that moment, STRATA didn't exist. I hadn't built the framework yet, but something shifted. I stopped asking if they'd accept me, and I started asking, "What signal do *I* want to send?"

That one question changed everything. Instead of trying to match *their* expectations, I matched *my* intention. I walked into the room like I belonged there. Not because of credentials or confidence, but because I had something to give, and I was done waiting to be picked.

That's the final transfer. The moment where you stop seeking influence... and start *embodying* it. This isn't just about business. Or sales. Or communication. This is about how you decide to be seen.

Do you enter rooms trying to prove your worth? Or do you enter rooms knowing your signal will do the work for you? Do you speak in a way that invites performance? Or do you speak in a way that demands presence?

STRATA doesn't give you a script. It gives you the *authority* to show up unscripted. Once you know how to read people, name their needs, flip their frame, and embed the moment, you don't need to rely on pressure or persuasion. You just need to show up clear. Posture does the rest.

So this is your call forward:

If you've ever felt like you had something to say but didn't know how to say it...

If you've ever walked away from a conversation knowing you missed the moment...

If you've ever watched someone else take credit for an idea you had but didn't claim...

Let STRATA be your tool to take it back. Not with noise. But with *nerve*. The kind of quiet clarity that flips power dynamics without having to shout. The kind of presence that moves people before you even open your mouth.

You don't need permission to use this. You already earned it by living the moments this book describes. So go back into your business. Into your leadership. Into your conversations. But this time, do it knowing you can:

- Read the unspoken.
- Pivot the frame.
- Anchor the belief.
- Transfer the power.
- And move the moment.

That's STRATA. Not just a framework. Not just a method. A way of showing up that turns invisible influence into visible results.

And now, my friend, it's your move. Let the world see the mind mechanic at work. Let them feel the STRATA shift. Because you don't just read people; you rewrite the moment.

# FINAL NOTE FROM THE AUTHOR

You now hold something most people will never possess. You can see the invisible architecture of every conversation, the signals that decide outcomes, the triggers that reveal the truth beneath the words, the pivots that shift a person's entire frame of reference. You no longer have to guess where a conversation is going. You can see it. You can feel it. And more importantly, you can change it.

This is the part no one teaches. They'll tell you to prepare your message, to polish your story, to choose the right words. But they won't show you how to read what's happening beneath the surface, in real time, and use it to create a connection that can't be faked. That's what STRATA gives you—a lens into the part of communication that shapes every deal closed, every relationship built, every moment of trust earned.

From here forward, you are no longer playing the same game as everyone else. While others are busy performing for the version of the room they *hope* is listening, you'll be speaking to the version that actually makes the decision. While they're explaining, you'll be adjusting. While they're guessing, you'll be certain.

Use this every day. Use it in the conversations that matter most and in the ones that seem routine. You'll start seeing patterns you've missed your entire life, and once you see them, you can't unsee them. That is your advantage. That is the work. And if you commit to it, the way you connect, influence, and lead will never look the same again. The room has always been talking. Now you understand the language.

# STRATA EXERCISES
# DECODE THE SIGNAL

While STRATA is a system that quickly allows you to communicate, influence, sell, and really be better with people, there is no magic bullet. Goethe said, "Knowing is not enough; we must apply. Willing is not enough; we must do." With this in in mind, the following sections allow you to begin to see STRATA in action. This first section shows examples of decoding the signal. Each exercise highlights a real-world scenario, identifies what the signal is, and offers a solution you can take to address the issue.

## Exercise 1

### Scenario:

You're pitching to a VP of Sales. As you speak, she leans back slightly, tilts her head, and presses her lips together. She says, "Interesting," but doesn't ask any follow-up questions.

### What's the signal?

Mild disengagement masked as politeness.

## Solution:

The lean back and lip press suggest hesitation or doubt. "Interesting" is a classic *non-committal deflection*. This is not curiosity, it's quiet rejection. Shift by saying: "I noticed I might've missed the mark. What part isn't resonating yet?"

## Exercise 2

## Scenario:

Your prospect folds their arms, but they're nodding along as you present. Their feet stay pointed toward you, and their brow is slightly furrowed.

## What's the signal?

Mental engagement with physical guardedness.

## Solution:

The nod and feet say "I'm here," but the arms and furrowed brow say "I'm still deciding." Don't overcorrect. Ask for their take: "I can tell you're thinking this through. What part are you wrestling with right now?"

# Exercise 3

## Scenario:

On a team call, one manager keeps glancing off-screen, typing occasionally, and delays a few seconds before responding. When they finally speak, their answer is generic and safe.

## What's the signal?

Divided attention. Low buy-in.

## Solution:

This person is checking out, not because they're busy, but because they're not bought in. Redirect with presence: "Hey, I want to make sure this is landing. Would it be helpful to pause and reset the frame?"

# Exercise 4

## Scenario:

You're in a heated discussion. The other person suddenly goes quiet, looking down and slightly away. They stop gesturing and give clipped, short answers like "Sure" and "Okay."

## What's the signal?

Withdrawal. You lost the room.

## Solution:

They've shut down, not because they agree, but because they've disengaged emotionally. You've likely hit a nerve. Back off with empathy: "I might've pushed too fast there. Want to take a step back for a second?"

## Exercise 5

### Scenario:

During a coaching session, a client says, "I guess I just need to be more confident," while smiling. Their tone is light, but their eyes dart sideways and their voice drops on the word "confident."

### What's the signal?

Discomfort cloaked in humor.

### Solution:

They're not stating a truth—they're trying to dodge the discomfort. The smile is a mask. Go underneath: "When you say 'be more confident,' what's the real story under that smile?"

# Exercise 6

## Scenario:

At a networking event, someone's telling you about their company. They keep adjusting their watch, scanning the room, and wrapping up sentences quickly, even though they say they "love meeting people."

## What's the signal?

Social anxiety or desire to exit.

## Solution:

This person is looking for a way out. Their signals are escape-oriented. Don't trap them; offer the out: "Hey, I'm glad we connected. Want to circle back later, or keep this short for now?"

# Exercise 7

## Scenario:

You ask a stakeholder if they're ready to move forward. They respond with a forced chuckle and say, "You know how these things go..." while scratching the back of their neck.

## What's the signal?

Avoidance. Anxiety response.

## Solution:

The scratch and chuckle are classic tells for internal friction. They're uncomfortable saying no. Make it easier: "Totally fair. It sounds like timing's not right. Want to talk next steps on your end?"

## Exercise 8

## Scenario:

In a brainstorm, someone cuts you off to finish your sentence—twice. They lean forward, speak rapidly, and seem excited but slightly aggressive.

## What's the signal?

Control impulse disguised as enthusiasm.

## Solution:

They're not just engaged, they're trying to steer. You can either anchor and redirect or let them lead for a bit. Try: "Love the energy. Want to build this out together or want me to lay out the full thought first?"

## Exercise 9

## Scenario:

Your teenager says they're "fine" after a rough day but won't make eye contact, shoulders are slumped, and their bag is still half-on when they try to leave the room.

## What's the signal?

Emotional residue. Not fine at all.

## Solution:

The body says what the words won't. Don't confront, connect: "You don't have to talk about it now, but I can tell something's still heavy. I'm here when you're ready."

## Exercise 10

## Scenario:

During a Zoom call, a client shifts from camera-on to camera-off without warning. When they come back, their tone is flatter, and their responses shorter.

## What's the signal?

Posture collapse. Something shifted.

## Solution:

Something happened—internal or external—and they're now guarded. Re-open gently: "We had good momentum before. Just checking in. Did something shift for you just now?"

## Wrap-Up: Building Your Signal Intuition

The scenarios, signal identifiers, and solution in this practice chapter aren't tricks or canned formulas, they're training reps. Real-time influence doesn't come from a script, it comes from fluency. From noticing the slight lean, the flicker in the tone, the pause that wasn't there five minutes ago. From treating people not as obstacles, but as signals waiting to be read.

Keep practicing. Not to control people, but to connect better, move smarter, and make the moment count.

# STRATA EXERCISES

# SPOT THE TRIGGER

This section of exercises shows examples of how to spot the trigger. Each exercise highlights a real-world scenario, identifies what the trigger is, and offers a solution you can take to address the issue.

## Exercise 1

### Scenario:

A founder says, "I'm not sure we're ready for that level of exposure yet," after you suggest a major PR opportunity. He keeps his arms crossed and glances toward his co-founder.

### What's the Trigger?

Fear of being judged or not having full control.

### Solution:

This isn't about exposure—it's about *exposure of weakness*. The founder feels uncertain about readiness and doesn't want to risk the brand. You're bumping up against a **control trigger**. Instead of pushing the opportunity, acknowledge: "Totally get that—sounds like staying in control of the story matters more than just visibility right now."

## Exercise 2

### Scenario:

A team lead says, "We've tried that before," with a tight jaw and flat tone after you suggest a new workflow system.

### What's the Trigger?

Fear of wasted effort and emotional exhaustion.

### Solution:

They're not just skeptical, they're tired of failed initiatives. The **fatigue trigger** is active. You'll make no progress until you validate that exhaustion. You can say something like this: "I can tell this isn't the first time someone's pitched a fix. How'd the last one go south?"

## Exercise 3

### Scenario:

Your spouse says, "Fine. Do whatever you want," but their voice is clipped and they walk away without waiting for a response.

## What's the Trigger?

Abandonment or loss of influence.

## Solution:

This isn't apathy; it's a protest withdrawal. The **significance trigger** is flaring. They don't feel seen or considered. Re-enter by addressing the deeper need: "I think I bulldozed your input there. That wasn't okay. Let's go back and do this together."

## Exercise 4

## Scenario:

A peer laughs when you share a new idea in a meeting and says, "You're always coming up with something wild."

## What's the Trigger?

Status preservation and fear of relevance loss.

## Solution:

That laugh wasn't friendly; it was protective. You just stepped into their turf, and now the **status trigger** is active. Lower the threat by inviting collaboration: "Totally fair. Want to poke holes in this with me and see if it holds?"

# Exercise 5

## Scenario:

You give performance feedback to a colleague. They nod, then launch into a list of everything they've been doing lately, including late nights and extra duties.

## What's the Trigger?

Fear of inadequacy or not being valued.

## Solution:

This is a **worth trigger**. They're hearing, "You're not enough." Defensiveness is their way of clawing back dignity. Pause and reset the frame: "What I said wasn't a question of effort. I can see you're going all in. This is about helping you get the results you deserve."

# Exercise 6

## Scenario:

In a sales conversation, a prospect says, "I need to run this by the team," despite previously saying they were the final decision-maker.

## What's the Trigger?

Risk aversion and fear of accountability.

## Solution:

This is a **responsibility trigger**. They're second-guessing the call, scared to own a mistake. Don't challenge the authority, normalize the fear. "Smart to pressure test this. What part still feels like a leap?"


## Exercise 7


## Scenario:

You suggest a partner try something new in their routine. They stiffen, go silent for a beat, and then say, "Why are you always trying to change me?"


## What's the Trigger?

Fear of rejection or being unlovable.


## Solution:

You tripped a **self-worth trigger**. The suggestion landed not as help, but as critique. Ease the signal by reinforcing safety: "This isn't about changing you. It's about supporting what *you* want. If this doesn't feel right, let's leave it."


## Exercise 8


## Scenario:

In a feedback session, a manager says, "I've been doing this for 15 years," after being questioned by a younger employee.

## What's the Trigger?

Fear of obsolescence or loss of expertise.

## Solution:

This is pure **legacy trigger**. They're defending experience because they feel it's being questioned. The antidote is recognition. "Fifteen years means you've seen the cycles. That's why your input matters. What's the long-view here?"

## Exercise 9

## Scenario:

You express concern about a friend's business. They immediately say, "You don't believe in me, do you?" with a sharp edge in their voice.

## What's the Trigger?

Fear of betrayal and need for loyalty.

## Solution:

This is the **loyalty trigger** lighting up. They're interpreting concern as doubt. Don't reassure. Reconnect. "I'm in your corner so hard I don't want to watch you walk into a buzzsaw. Can we talk about what I'm seeing?"

# Exercise 10

## Scenario:

In a strategy meeting, someone repeatedly interrupts, insists on their plan, and cuts others off with phrases like, "Trust me, this is the way."

## What's the Trigger?

Loss of control or fear of chaos.

## Solution:

That urgency isn't just passion; it's the **control trigger** panicking. The tighter they grip, the more threatened they feel. Give them some, but not all of, the reins: "Let's run with your approach, but build in a checkpoint after week one so we can adapt if needed."

## Wrap-Up: From Reactivity to Insight

Every Trigger is a tell. Not a weakness. Not a flaw. Just a signpost that someone is trying to protect something important. Mastering Trigger means recognizing that behavior is never random. It's responsive. It's layered. And the person you're talking with isn't fighting you, they're fighting the risk of *being exposed*.

You're not there to tear the shield away. You're there to understand why it's there... and what it would take for them to lower it themselves. That's what makes STRATA surgical. And that's what makes you a mind mechanic.

# STRATA EXERCISES

# REFRAME – FLIP THE LENS WITHOUT FORCE

This section of exercises shows examples of how to spot something that needs to be reframed. Each exercise highlights a real-world scenario, offers how you can reframe if necessary, and provides an explanation of the reframe.

## Exercise 1

### Scenario:

A project manager says, "I don't have time to teach them. I might as well do it myself."

### What's the Reframe?

"Sounds like you're not just trying to hit deadlines; you're trying to protect quality."

## Explanation:

This isn't laziness. It's pride in execution. The Reframe shifts it from micromanagement to guardianship. You've now created space for the idea that teaching *is* quality protection.

## Exercise 2

## Scenario:

A startup founder says, "We can't afford to slow down, not even for a second."

## What's the Reframe?

"I hear that speed is your edge. So the real risk is burning out your advantage by sprinting on a broken ankle."

## Explanation:

You align with the *value*—speed—before reframing the *risk* as hidden self-sabotage. Now slowing down becomes *strategic*, not *hesitant*.

## Exercise 3

## Scenario:

A rep says, "This client just doesn't get it. They're impossible."

## What's the Reframe?

"Sounds like they're not impossible; they're just operating on a completely different playbook."

## Explanation:

You remove the blame and introduce *curiosity*. Instead of fighting the client, the rep is now challenged to decode them. That shifts frustration into motivation.

## Exercise 4

## Scenario:

A parent says, "I just don't want my kid to make the same mistakes I did."

## What's the Reframe?

"So this isn't about control. It's about giving them the head start you never got."

## Explanation:

You shift the story from overbearing to protective. It removes the guilt from the parent's intensity and gives them a new language for guidance.

# Exercise 5

## Scenario:

A senior leader says, "This team is too new. I can't rely on them yet."

## What's the Reframe?

"Sounds like your instinct is to protect the standard, and that means figuring out where to build trust, not just wait for it."

## Explanation:

You're naming the *intention* (high standards), and flipping the behavior from passive judgment to active development.

# Exercise 6

## Scenario:

A client says, "We've always done it this way. It works."

## What's the Reframe?

"I can see why you'd protect something that's working. What if we didn't replace it, just *repositioned* it to keep that same result faster?"

## Explanation:

You don't argue. You preserve the win and open a new path. This is reframing as *augmentation*, not *correction*.

## Exercise 7

## Scenario:

A salesperson says, "They ghosted me after our third meeting. No idea why."

## What's the Reframe?

"Maybe it wasn't rejection; it was confusion. They didn't ghost *you*. They ghosted the decision."

## Explanation:

You reframe it from personal failure to clarity gap. That changes the rep's posture from wounded to curious and gives them permission to re-engage *without shame*.

## Exercise 8

## Scenario:

A CEO says, "We need people who are hungry, not just clocking in."

## What's the Reframe?

"So you're not just hiring for skills, you're hiring for appetite. Which means the interview needs to show you who *wants to build*, not just do."

## Explanation:

Now hiring becomes an energy filter, not just a resume check. You've taken a complaint and turned it into a strategic calibration.

## Exercise 9

## Scenario:

An executive says, "I'm just not a 'camera person.' I hate the way I look and sound."

## What's the Reframe?

"So it's not about camera comfort; it's about message control. You want to be *in control* of how you show up."

## Explanation:

You normalize the discomfort and make it about *precision*, not *insecurity*. Now the next step isn't exposure, it's *refinement*.

# Exercise 10

## Scenario:

A coaching client says, "I keep starting things but I never finish. Maybe I'm just not wired for follow-through."

## What's the Reframe?

"Or maybe you're wired to chase momentum, and no one ever showed you how to sustain it without pressure."

## Explanation:

You detach their identity from the behavior. It's not a flaw. It's an unmet skill. That opens the door for possibility instead of shame.

## Wrap-Up: Reframing Is Redirection, Not Correction

Every Reframe starts with permission. You're not negating their reality; you're revealing a better lens. And when done right, it doesn't feel like strategy. It feels like **relief.** Like you've finally given them a story they can believe in *and* act on.

The power of Reframe isn't in clever wordplay. It's in emotional clarity. You're not trying to convince someone they're wrong. You're showing them how they were right, just in the wrong direction.

And once that lands, you don't have to push the conversation anymore. They'll *pull it forward.*

# STRATA EXERCISES

# ANCHOR – MAKING IT STICK

This section of exercises shows examples of how to spot something that needs an anchor. Each exercise highlights a real-world scenario, offers how you can create an anchor to make something stick, and provides an explanation of the anchor.

## Exercise 1

### Scenario:

A sales leader finally gets their team aligned on messaging, but two weeks later, everyone's back to winging it.

### What Anchor could make it stick?

"Remember how it *felt* when the whole team said the same thing, and the client leaned in like they'd been waiting for it all day?"

### Explanation:

You're not anchoring a *concept*; you're anchoring a *feeling*. The moment of team sync is emotional fuel. Make them relive it so they can return to effectiveness. Anchor = emotional memory + ownership.

## Exercise 2

### Scenario:

A founder keeps hesitating to pitch investors. They say it's not "the right time."

### What Anchor could make it stick?

"You didn't build this out of safety. You built it out of refusal, because no one else saw it. *That's* the pitch."

### Explanation:

You tie the idea to an *emotional origin story*. The anchor here is identity: this wasn't built cautiously; it was born out of rebellion. That makes movement feel aligned, not risky.

## Exercise 3

### Scenario:

A parent is hesitant to enforce boundaries with their teen, worried they'll damage the relationship.

### What Anchor could make it stick?

"What if the boundary *is* the love? The part that says, 'I see who you're becoming, and I'm going to protect that version of you, even when you fight me.'"

## Explanation:

You're anchoring the discomfort in *devotion*. It's not control. It's investment in who that child will become. Anchor the hard choice to a deeper value.

## Exercise 4

## Scenario:

A client doesn't want to fire a toxic employee who's harming the team.

## What Anchor could make it stick?

"Keeping them is a vote *against* everyone else who shows up right. And you're telling them effort doesn't matter."

## Explanation:

You create *emotional cost*, not theoretical risk. The anchor is guilt reoriented toward the *right person*. You're showing what it signals to the team.

## Exercise 5

## Scenario:

A coaching client says, "I know I should be more visible, but I don't want to seem arrogant."

## What Anchor could make it stick?

"Visibility isn't vanity. It's responsibility. If the right people can't find you, they'll end up trusting someone who doesn't care."

## Explanation:

You link the behavior (visibility) to *moral obligation*. Anchoring works best when it makes inaction feel selfish and action feel *protective*.

## Exercise 6

## Scenario:

An executive team finally agrees to pivot their product strategy, but there's hesitation.

## What Anchor could make it stick?

"We're not changing course. We're *correcting aim*. And no one remembers the guy who stayed the course when the map was wrong."

## Explanation:

You anchor it to *precision*, not panic. Now the pivot feels like leadership, not retreat. Anchors protect ego while introducing momentum.

# Exercise 7

## Scenario:

A team member resists public speaking, saying, "I'm just not built for it."

## What Anchor could make it stick?

"Neither are most people, but that moment where someone hears *your exact words* and finally gets it? That's what you're built for."

## Explanation:

Anchor the behavior to a *human moment*, not a label. You're not fixing them, you're unlocking a version of them they already care about.

# Exercise 8

## Scenario:

A founder keeps changing direction and says, "I just get excited about new ideas."

## What Anchor could make it stick?

"That excitement's not the problem; it's your *fuel*. But if you don't ground it, you're setting sparks to dry grass."

## Explanation:

Anchor = containment, not cancellation. You're not stripping their excitement; you're reframing its *application* so it doesn't burn out progress.

## Exercise 9

## Scenario:

A manager is micromanaging their team but says, "I just want to make sure it gets done right."

## What Anchor could make it stick?

"What if your *trust* is what gets it done right? What if you showing belief is the most instructional thing you can offer?"

## Explanation:

You take the root desire—*doing it right*—and anchor it to a different behavior: *letting go*. It redefines control as *trust-building*.

## Exercise 10

## Scenario:

A client hesitates to raise their rates. "I don't want to scare people off."

## What Anchor could make it stick?

"If your price doesn't make someone sit up straight, you're not in the room you're supposed to be in."

## Explanation:

You re-anchor value perception. Pricing becomes signal. Not about greed, about *right fit*. You make confidence the protective posture.

## Wrap-Up: Anchors Aren't Reminders. They're Emotional Handholds.

The whole point of STRATA is to shift behavior without force. Anchor is the moment that shift *sticks*. Because logic doesn't hold in tension, emotion *does*. Every insight needs weight. A reason to *feel* true, not just sound right.

Anchors come in three forms:

- **Emotion seals it.**
- **Ownership cements it.**
- **Context protects it.**

Use their past to prove the insight, their identity to hold the insight, and their environment to defend the insight. That's how you create a *behavioral reflex*, not just a cognitive nod.

When you anchor well, the person doesn't just agree with you, they *repeat it to others*. And that's when you know it's no longer yours—it *lives in them*.

# STRATA EXERCISES

# TRANSFER — MAKE IT THEIRS

This section of exercises shows examples of how to spot something that needs a transfer. Each exercise highlights a real-world scenario, offers how you can use a transfer, and provides an explanation of why the transfer is effective.

## Exercise 1

### Scenario:

You've just given a great strategic suggestion to your client. They say "That's interesting," but nothing changes.

### What Transfer move could you use?

"Let me pause. How would *you* describe what's not working right now? Because I think it's already something you've been sensing."

### Explanation:

You shift from telling to reflecting. Transfer happens when *they connect their own dots*. You're not giving answers; you're giving them back *their own insight* with clearer language.

# Exercise 2

## Scenario:

A team agrees with your pitch in the meeting, but no one champions it after the call.

## What Transfer move could you use?

"Can you help me shape this for the next conversation? I want it to reflect your team's voice, not just mine."

## Explanation:

This invites co-ownership. Transfer needs fingerprints. When they help shape the message, they'll defend it like it's *theirs*. Ownership precedes advocacy.

# Exercise 3

## Scenario:

A founder says "I get it," but still keeps clinging to old habits that don't scale.

## What Transfer move could you use?

"Walk me through how you'd explain this shift to your team. What would you say if this were your idea from the beginning?"

## Explanation:

You're triggering *mental rehearsal.* When someone explains something in their own words, it moves from echo to embodiment. Transfer isn't passive; it's *personal rehearsal.*

## Exercise 4

## Scenario:

A leader tells you they're aligned with the culture change, but they're still using old language and metrics.

## What Transfer move could you use?

"Let's pick one phrase your team hears every week. What if we tweaked that to reflect the new direction? Something that sounds like you but lands differently?"

## Explanation:

Transfer lives in language. Culture isn't a memo, it's repetition. Microshifts in phrasing often create macroshifts in perception. Get *their* voice into the new frame.

## Exercise 5

## Scenario:

You're coaching someone through a difficult realization. They intellectually agree, but they look away when they say it.

## What Transfer move could you use?

"Say that again but this time like you were telling it to someone who needed to hear it."

## Explanation:

Transfer often needs a *proxy*. Saying it as advice to someone else reduces self-defense. Once they own it out loud, it loops back as internal truth.

## Exercise 6

## Scenario:

You're helping someone improve their messaging. You give them a new angle and they nod, but don't update the copy.

## What Transfer move could you use?

"What if you wrote the first three lines like *you were already winning*, like you didn't need to prove anything?"

## Explanation:

Transfer requires an *emotional shift*, not just a tactical one. You're asking them to *step into* the identity that holds the message. Embodiment beats compliance.

# Exercise 7

## Scenario:

You explain a team dynamic perfectly. The manager agrees but still keeps blaming one employee.

## What Transfer move could you use?

"I know I laid that out, but where do *you* see it? What pattern have you been noticing that maybe hasn't had words until now?"

## Explanation:

You reorient credit. Let them excavate the insight themselves. When they uncover it, they protect it. Transfer is about discovery, not delivery.

# Exercise 8

## Scenario:

You're training a group, and one participant finally gets it but their body language says, "This isn't mine to say."

## What Transfer move could you use?

"You just said something that stopped the room. Can you say that again, louder?"

## Explanation:

Spotlight creates transfer. When you reflect their power back to them and invite them to *own the moment*, they begin to internalize authority.

## Exercise 9

## Scenario:

You're pitching a framework to a client, and they love it, but they keep calling it "your method."

## What Transfer move could you use?

"What would you rename this if it were part of your onboarding? I want the name that *feels like you*."

## Explanation:

Renaming is reframing. Giving it their label breaks the ownership wall. The more their language embeds, the more they *feel responsible* for it.

## Exercise 10

## Scenario:

You've helped a founder shape a new go-to-market strategy. It's good, but they still say, "We'll try it and see."

## What Transfer move could you use?

"If it works, who do you think it helps first? Not the customer, the person inside the team who's been waiting for this?"

## Explanation:

Now it's *personal*. You're transferring not the idea but the *impact*. You link the strategy to someone they care about, making the shift emotionally real.

## Wrap-Up: Transfer Is the Pivot from Agreement to Ownership

You don't move people by making great points; you move them by making it *feel like theirs*. That's why Transfer isn't step one. It comes *after* the Signal has been read, the Trigger understood, the Frame shifted, and the Anchor embedded.

At this point, they're not resisting you; they're almost ready to run with it. But not until it stops sounding like *your language*.

Transfer techniques work because they...

- Invite participation
- Rehearse ownership
- Mirror values
- Align language
- And shrink the distance between *their world* and *your insight*

Remember: Influence ends the second they feel like it's your idea. But when they take it personally? They fight for it. They *repeat* it. They *refine* it. And eventually... They forget you ever said it at all. Which is exactly the point.

# STRATA EXERCISES
# ACTION — MAKING IT REAL

This section of exercises shows examples of how to spot something that needs a transfer. Each exercise highlights a real-world scenario, offers how you can us an action move, and provides an explanation of why the action move is effective.

## Exercise 1

### Scenario:

You've walked your client through the new strategy. They nod, say it makes sense, then end the call without committing.

### What Action move could you use?

"Let's not leave this theoretical. What's the first move you'd want your team making by Thursday?"

### Explanation:

You're shortening the distance between belief and behavior. Abstract agreement becomes irrelevant without a near-term next step. Anchor them to a clear, specific action window.

# Exercise 2

## Scenario:

A rep finishes your training session energized but when asked what they'll change on their next call, they freeze.

## What Action move could you use?

"Picture your next call. What's one line you'd say differently if you were already closing like a top performer?"

## Explanation:

Action often needs rehearsal. You're prompting them to simulate forward, to feel themselves succeeding before they move. Behavior begins with visualized readiness.

# Exercise 3

## Scenario:

You're advising a founder who wants to "think on it" for another week even though they've already expressed full alignment.

## What Action move could you use?

"Totally fair. And if you *didn't* wait—if you moved now—what would that unlock this month that waiting wouldn't?"

## Explanation:

This removes pressure while reframing urgency. You're not pushing; you're illuminating opportunity cost. When the moment matters, delay is a decision.

## Exercise 4

## Scenario:

A buyer says, "This sounds great. We'll loop back next quarter."

## What Action move could you use?

"Before we punt this to Q4, what would make it feel like a *now* decision—not for me, but for your team's momentum?"

## Explanation:

Great action prompts reclaim priority. You're shifting the lens from you to them. When they define urgency, it's theirs to honor.

## Exercise 5

## Scenario:

You just helped someone break through a fear in coaching, but they're hesitant to commit to the change they said they wanted.

## What Action move could you use?

"Let's test the belief. What's one thing you'd do differently in the next 48 hours if that fear didn't run the show?"

## Explanation:

You're not pushing them to be fearless. You're asking them to behave as if the shift already happened. Action flows from identity, not willpower.

## Exercise 6

## Scenario:

Your team agrees on a new outreach strategy, but the calendar's blank and no one's scheduled a session.

## What Action move could you use?

"Whose calendar do we drop this on first? I'll join if needed but it needs a name and a time before we leave this room."

## Explanation:

You're anchoring action in logistics. Abstract approval is a stall tactic. Great leaders remove fog by forcing calendar-level clarity.

# Exercise 7

## Scenario:

A client says they'll "try out" your idea but you can feel the hesitation in their voice.

## What Action move could you use?

"What's the smallest version of this you could test today, just to feel it in motion?"

## Explanation:

Big leaps freeze people. But micro-moves create momentum. When you scale the ask down to feel doable, you lower the psychological cost of starting.

# Exercise 8

## Scenario:

Someone's inspired by your keynote and comes up to say "This really made me think." They start walking away.

## What Action move could you use?

"If you let that thought change something today, what would it be?"

## Explanation:

You're interrupting passive consumption. Insight is nice but impact requires reflection turned into motion. You bring the shift into their day, not just their mind.

## Exercise 9

## Scenario:

You've just wrapped a pitch and the prospect says, "Let us think about it as a team."

## What Action move could you use?

"Absolutely. Can I send a single-sentence summary of what I think you're saying yes to, just to make sure we're moving forward on the same page?"

## Explanation:

You're creating a soft close. It's non-threatening, but subtly moves them toward a shared commitment. Friction lowers when clarity rises.

## Exercise 10

## Scenario:

Your mentee has been stuck in planning mode for weeks refining a strategy they say they believe in, but never launching.

# What Action move could you use?

"You've earned the plan. Now what's the move that says, 'This is real now?' Doesn't have to be big, just something that makes the future feel started."

# Explanation:

Perfection often masks fear. You're offering a reframe: that action doesn't require certainty—just initiation. It's a behavioral green light.

# Wrap-Up: Action Is the Bridge Between Insight and Reality

Insight without movement is just decoration. Action is where belief turns into behavior. It's the moment that takes everything you've read, reframed, and anchored, and locks it into the real world. The key isn't pushing harder; it's shrinking the gap between "I get it" and "I did it."

Great Action moves work because they...

- • Collapse time - moving decisions closer.
- • Scale effort - breaking the impossible into the doable.
- • Test identity - asking people to behave as if the shift already happened.
- • Anchor logistics - tying the change to calendars, names, and steps.

Remember: people don't change when they *understand* something. They change when they *move differently* because of it. Action is where the loop closes. When you can get someone to take even the smallest next step, the bigger ones follow and the strategy isn't theory anymore, it's real.

# APPENDIX 1

# STRATA IN THE WILD: REAL-WORLD EXAMPLES OF BEHAVIORAL CUES

Sometimes the most powerful STRATA moments don't happen in boardrooms, sales calls, or scripted presentations. They happen at the dinner table. In a waiting room. During a checkout line pause. In a group chat. These are the moments where cues get leaked, posture collapses, tension surfaces, and conversations shift without anyone realizing why.

This section is about recognizing STRATA in the wild. Each example is short, sharp, and designed to hit you with a moment you've either lived or witnessed and then name the layer at play, the cue that tipped it, and the move that could've shifted the moment.

## At the Doctor's Office

You finally get called back. The doctor walks in, greets you without making eye contact, opens their laptop, and starts typing.

Layer: Signal

Cue: No eye contact, typing while greeting

Interpretation: Disconnection, lack of presence

STRATA Move: Pause. Don't jump into your symptoms. Match their rhythm by holding eye contact and waiting. Let your stillness signal this deserves attention.

## Zoom Team Meeting

You propose an idea. One team member exhales through their nose and leans back slightly. Nothing is said, but the energy just shifted.

Layer: Trigger

Cue: Exhale + lean back

Interpretation: Subtle pushback or skepticism

STRATA Move: Reframe. Name the moment lightly, "Sounds like there's some hesitation. Want to poke holes in it?" Invite their resistance out instead of ignoring it.

## Family Dinner

Your teenager answers a question with "I said I'd do it" but their volume dips, eyes roll, and they look away.

Layer: Trigger

Cue: Muted response plus eye roll

Interpretation: Passive resistance, signal misalignment

STRATA Move: Anchor. Match the emotional state and re-establish connection, "Hey, I'm not trying to corner you. Can we talk about it without the eye roll?"

## Date Night

You ask your partner if they're okay. They say "I'm fine," but their arms are crossed and their body is turned away.

Layer: Signal

Cue: Arms crossed plus body turned

Interpretation: Emotional shutdown, protective stance

STRATA Move: Reframe. Don't argue the words; acknowledge the posture. "I hear you, but your body's saying something else. Want to tell me what's actually going on?"


## Group Chat

A normally active friend leaves your comment unread. Others respond. They don't. Later, they post in a different group.

Layer: Transfer

Cue: Selective silence

Interpretation: Withholding engagement, boundary shift

STRATA Move: Action. Don't chase; name the change. "Hey, just checking. Did I say something off? I noticed you didn't jump in like usual."

# APPENDIX 2

# STRATA DAILY PRACTICES

## Signal

1. Walk into a room and pay attention to how you carry yourself—relaxed shoulders, steady breathing, and eye contact. Notice how people respond before you speak.

2. Start a Zoom call by pausing for one full breath before speaking. Let others speak first and observe their initial energy and posture.

3. Record yourself making a short intro (30 seconds). Watch it back and take note of your tone, rhythm, and posture. Adjust and try again.

4. Speak one-on-one with someone and consciously mirror their tone and tempo—not mimic, but align with it subtly.

5. When telling a story or giving a quick update, vary your tone and pace intentionally. See how it feels to slow down when emphasizing something important.

# Trigger

6. Ask someone a casual question and observe the first 2 seconds of their reaction. Was there hesitation, deflection, or tightening in their face?

7. Notice your own shift when someone disagrees with you. Does your tone harden? Do you lean in or back away?

8. Practice staying neutral when someone shares a problem. Don't jump to solve—just acknowledge and explore their emotional signal.

9. During a conversation, say something slightly unexpected (but not inappropriate) and watch for changes in facial expression or posture.

10. Listen to someone vent and try to spot the moment where emotion spikes—this is often where the real trigger lives.


# Reframe

11. Take a complaint someone gives you today and reframe it as a need or desire. (Example: 'This is too hard' becomes 'You want a simpler process.')

12. Practice saying, 'So what I'm hearing is...' and rephrase what the other person said to check if you understood their meaning.

13. When you feel frustrated or stuck, write down how you're seeing the situation. Then rewrite it from three different perspectives (coach, ally, opponent).

14. Watch a 2-minute news clip or ad and reframe the core message into something emotionally opposite. (Confidence → doubt, problem → power)

15. During a disagreement, pause and ask, 'What would this sound like if we were both on the same side already?'

# Anchor

16. When someone shares a strong emotion, pause and reflect it back: 'That sounds really frustrating' or 'That must've felt good.'

17. Use a physical cue like placing your hand on the table or nodding when emphasizing something—see how it lands differently.

18. Think of a time you felt strong and calm. Anchor yourself in that state before going into a conversation that matters.

19. Tell a story today that meant something to you. Watch how the listener responds, especially when you pause at key moments.

20. Repeat someone's key phrase back to them. Let it hang in the air without adding your opinion. Feel how the room shifts.

# Transfer

21. After sharing an idea, ask 'What do you think?' or 'How does that land with you?' Notice how the energy moves back to them.

22. Practice saying 'If this were already working, what would be different?' to help someone take ownership of change.

23. Wrap up a conversation with, 'What's the one thing you're taking from this?'—observe how clearly or vaguely they answer.

24. Look for opportunities to say, 'Here's how I see it, but you tell me where it lands differently for you.'

25. Before giving advice or direction, ask, 'Are you open to a different way of seeing this?' Let them signal permission.

## Action

26. End each day by reflecting: *Where did I show up the way I intended? Where did I default?* Write one micro-adjustment for tomorrow.

27. After a key conversation, jot down one thing you could do differently next time — and one thing you nailed.

28. Before entering a meeting or call, define a single outcome you want to create — not control, but *influence.*

29. Choose one behavior you noticed in someone else today and test it yourself tomorrow. Observe what changes.

30. End each week by asking yourself, *What felt easier now than it did a week ago?* Track your progress — that's your signal the system is working.

# APPENDIX 3

# STRATA CUE AND TELL SUMMARY

This glossary is a practical field guide for reading real-time behavioral cues.

Each cue maps to a layer of STRATA—**Signal, Trigger, Reframe, Anchor, Transfer, or Action**—and helps you see what's really happening beneath the surface of a conversation.

The goal isn't to overanalyze; it's to *notice, interpret, and respond* with precision.

---

Signal

## 1. Sudden glance at a watch or phone

**Interpretation:** Their mind has moved on. You've either lost urgency or over-explained. This isn't disrespect—it's disengagement.

**STRATA Move:** Match pace. Either accelerate to the point or pause and check in: "Is this still the right time to finish this?" You'll often reengage them simply by naming the shift.

## 2. Crossed arms with a relaxed face

**Interpretation:** They're not defensive—they're protecting attention. This is containment, not rejection.

**STRATA Move:** Reopen body language with mirroring or movement. Step forward slightly, change posture, or hand them something to hold. Movement resets energy.

## 3. Shrinking posture (hunched shoulders, tucked chin)

**Interpretation:** They feel smaller in the moment—outmatched, uncertain, or under pressure.

**STRATA Move:** Anchor safety through tone and body openness. Lower your voice, slow your tempo, and create space for them to step back in.

## 4. Rapid blinking or rubbing eyes

**Interpretation:** They're overloaded—too much information or emotion too fast.

**STRATA Move:** Stop talking. Ask one grounding question like, "What's landing most right now?" Silence allows recalibration.

## 5. Steepled fingers

**Interpretation:** This is a confidence cue—they're asserting control, testing whether you're equally grounded.

**STRATA Move:** Match calm authority. Keep posture steady, acknowledge their insight, and reframe toward collaboration: "Exactly—here's how we could build on that."

## 6. Voice pitch rising mid-conversation

**Interpretation:** Rising pitch signals internal pressure—trying to prove, defend, or be validated.

**STRATA Move:** Lower your own tone and slow your rhythm. Your calm voice will subconsciously restore balance to the interaction.

---

## Trigger

## 1. Crossed arms paired with a tight jaw

**Interpretation:** Classic defense cue—they've felt cornered or judged. It's not hostility; it's protection.

**STRATA Move:** Ease pressure. Shift from proving to exploring: "You're right to question that—let's walk it through together."

## 2. Looking away while agreeing

**Interpretation:** Verbal yes, emotional no. They're preserving harmony, not commitment.

**STRATA Move:** Reengage curiosity. "You hesitated a second—what's on your mind?" That single permission can surface the truth.

## 3. Interrupting repeatedly

**Interpretation:** A control signal. They're anxious to regain footing or steer the direction.

**STRATA Move:** Ground the room. Pause, then calmly say, "Let's finish this thread, then I'm all yours." That validates control without surrendering flow.

## 4. Exaggerated agreement ("Exactly! Yes! 100%!" too soon)

**Interpretation:** They're agreeing to move on, not because they believe it. Often masks impatience or discomfort.

**STRATA Move:** Slow the tempo. Ask for nuance: "I like that enthusiasm—what part resonates most?" It reveals depth or lack thereof.

## 5. Tight jaw with a forced smile

**Interpretation:** Conflict suppression—they're swallowing disagreement.

**STRATA Move:** Give them a safe exit. "You don't have to agree—I'm more interested in how you see it." Authenticity beats false harmony.

## 6. Repeating the same phrase or question

**Interpretation:** Internal resistance—trying to process something they don't fully accept yet.

**STRATA Move:** Reframe the language. Simplify the idea or restate it emotionally: "It sounds like what you're really weighing is whether it's worth the risk."

# Reframe

## 1. Sudden pause after a statement

**Interpretation:** They've hit internal conflict—something didn't sit right, but they're deciding whether to voice it.

**STRATA Move:** Don't fill the silence. Wait, then ask gently, "What just came up for you?" That moment births honesty.

## 2. Tilted head and narrowed eyes

**Interpretation:** Curiosity mixed with skepticism—they're trying to reconcile what you said with what they believe.

**STRATA Move:** Join their doubt. "It sounds like you're testing that idea—what's the part that feels off?" You turn resistance into collaboration.

## 3. Small laugh after tension

**Interpretation:** A release valve—they're masking discomfort through humor.

**STRATA Move:** Acknowledge, then redirect: "I know it's funny, but it's also real, right?" Laughter fades, truth surfaces.

## 4. Echoing your words back with a question tone

**Interpretation:** They're replaying your point to test meaning—"Do I buy this?"

**STRATA Move:** Clarify, don't defend. "Yeah, that's exactly it—though in this case it means..." You keep control without overpowering.

## 5. Deflecting with logic after emotional content

**Interpretation:** They've retreated from emotion to safety. It's a pivot from vulnerability to intellect.

**STRATA Move:** Reconnect emotionally: "You went logical just now—what did that hit for you a second earlier?" It brings them back to authenticity.

---

## Anchor

## 1. Shallow breathing or visible tension in shoulders

**Interpretation:** They're flooded—trying to hold themselves together.

**STRATA Move:** Model calm. Slow your breath, drop your volume, and let silence expand. Your composure becomes the anchor.

## 2. Breaking eye contact mid-story

**Interpretation:** They've left the moment—emotion rising, memory triggered, or uncertainty surfacing.

**STRATA Move:** Hold space quietly. A gentle "Take your time" resets safety faster than any reassurance.

## 3. Overly controlled tone

**Interpretation:** They're performing composure, not feeling it. This is suppression disguised as professionalism.

**STRATA Move:** Mirror steadiness, then soften the edges. "You're staying incredibly calm—what's holding that together right now?" Naming it disarms the act.

## 4. Mirroring your words exactly

**Interpretation:** They're seeking stability through imitation—trying to re-sync energy.

**STRATA Move:** Slow down and let them catch rhythm naturally. Too much dominance keeps them dependent.

## 5. Hands or palms flat on the table

**Interpretation:** They're grounding themselves—literally anchoring to feel control.

**STRATA Move:** Match the gesture subtly, then redirect focus: "Feels like we both want this to stay steady—here's how we can do that."

---

Transfer

## 1. Asking "So what do you think?" too early

**Interpretation:** They're handing control back before you've landed your point.

**STRATA Move:** Don't take the bait—anchor first. "Let me finish one thought, then I want your take." You guide timing without power struggle.

## 2. Glancing at others before answering

**Interpretation:** Social permission check—they're gauging the room before speaking truth.

**STRATA Move:** Direct the focus back. "Forget everyone else—what's *your* read?" You free them from social constraint.


## 3. Leaning back with arms open

**Interpretation:** Transfer in progress—they're ready to receive or respond.

**STRATA Move:** Hand off with clarity: "So where does that land for you?" Ownership moves from you to them.


## 4. Long pause before answering a personal question

**Interpretation:** They're deciding how honest to be. Silence here means risk assessment, not disengagement.

**STRATA Move:** Validate the pause. "You don't have to rush that—I appreciate you thinking about it." It signals safety for real answers.


## 5. Nodding slowly while you speak

**Interpretation:** Processing agreement—not false compliance, but careful buy-in.

**STRATA Move:** Give them space to articulate it: "It looks like something clicked—want to put words to it?" Transfer completes through articulation.

# Action

## 1. Taking sudden notes mid-conversation

**Interpretation:** They've locked onto something actionable—it resonated enough to capture.

**STRATA Move:** Reinforce clarity: "That's worth noting—what stood out?" This cements commitment and lets them own the insight.

## 2. Leaning forward after prolonged stillness

**Interpretation:** Engagement spike—they're ready to move or decide.

**STRATA Move:** Land the ask immediately. "Sounds like you're ready—what's next step on your side?" Timing is everything.

## 3. Checking calendar or opening phone after agreement

**Interpretation:** They're mentally scheduling the follow-through.

**STRATA Move:** Support momentum. "Want to set a time now while it's fresh?" You convert intent to action before energy fades.

## 4. Sitting back with crossed ankles and soft face

**Interpretation:** Resolution. The tension's released, and they feel safe with the outcome.

**STRATA Move:** Acknowledge closure. "Feels like we're good here." Ending consciously preserves rapport for next time.

## 5. Hesitating before a handshake or closing gesture

**Interpretation:** Lingering uncertainty—they're still deciding if trust is earned.

**STRATA Move:** Don't push physical closure. Stay verbal: "No rush—I'll follow up with details." Respect gives reassurance, which seals the deal.

---

## Closing Note

These cues aren't meant to make you a human lie detector.

They're reminders that every room speaks twice—once in words, and again in signals.

STRATA helps you hear both at once, so you can meet people not just where they *are*, but where they're *stuck*.

When you learn to read the signal beneath the sentence, you stop talking to the performance and start leading the person.

# APPENDIX 4

# STRATA MAP TEMPLATE

Use this template to map a conversation, meeting, or interaction using the STRATA framework. Fill out each layer with what you observed, how you interpreted it, and what you did or could have done to adapt in real time.

## Signal

*What did you notice before anything was said? Think posture, tone, rhythm, urgency, presence.*

[Your notes here]

## Trigger

*What seemed to create a shift? Look for changes in energy, resistance, or emotional charge.*

[Your notes here]

## Reframe

---

*How did you or could you shift the meaning, change the lens, or defuse tension?*

---

[Your notes here]

## Anchor

---

*What belief or moment did you tie your message to? What stuck?*

---

[Your notes here]

## Transfer

---

*What permission, clarity, or shift in readiness did you create?*

---

[Your notes here]

## Action

---

*What was the outcome, and what behavior or next step was taken as a result?*

---

[Your notes here]

# ABOUT THE AUTHOR

Jake Stahl is known as *The Mind Mechanic*. A strategist, keynote speaker, and author dedicated to teaching people how to read others, command presence, and win the moments that matter most. Over the course of his career, Jake has trained more than 10,000 professionals across 47 states and six countries, helping sales teams, executives, and entrepreneurs stop being ignored and start becoming unforgettable.

He is the CEO and Co-Founder of **Orchestraight**, an AI-driven business development platform that operationalizes his proprietary Neurostrategy™ methodology. Built to help consultants, fractional executives, and enterprise teams refine their message and close more deals, Orchestraight has been recognized as a cutting-edge solution in strategic communication and business growth.

Jake's impact stretches beyond technology. He has led over 15 national product launches, holds seven patents in field-force sales technology, and has received the prestigious International Gold Award for Instructional Design. His STRATA framework, grounded in behavioral psychology, social psychology, and neuro-linguistic programming, has been credited with transforming how individuals and organizations communicate in real time.

Through his podcast *Own the Room*, keynote speeches, and workshops, Jake has become widely recognized as the man who can create the perfect conversation. His work has helped teams close multimillion-dollar accounts and leaders develop the presence to shift entire markets.

Jake lives in South Boston, Virginia, with his wife and their German shepherd, Kyrie. A proud father of four, he spends his free time traveling, attending NASCAR races, and helping entrepreneurs succeed in both business and life.

## Contact Jake

For interviews, keynote speaking, or consulting inquiries:

**Email:** Jake@Orchestraight.com

**Website:** www.thejakestahl.com

**LinkedIn:** https://www.linkedin.com/in/jakestahl

**TikTok:** @JaketheMindMechanic

**Instagram:** @JaketheMindMechanic

**YouTube:** @JaketheMindMechanic

**Podcast:** Own the Room with Jake Stahl

# DID YOU ENJOY THIS BOOK?

If you enjoyed reading this book, you can help by suggesting it to someone else you think might like it, and **please leave a positive review** wherever you purchased it. This does a lot in helping others find the book. We thank you in advance for taking a few moments to do this.

*THANK YOU*

## You might also like other Thin Leaf Press titles:

*Peak Performance: Mindset Tools for Managers*
*Peak Performance: Mindset Tools for Sales*
*Peak Performance: Mindset Tools for Leaders*
*Peak Performance: Mindset Tools for Business*
*Peak Performance: Mindset Tools for Entrepreneurs*
*Peak Performance: Mindset Tools for Athletes*
*The Successful Mind: Tools to Living a Purposeful, Productive, and Happy Life*
*The Successful Body: Using Fitness, Nutrition, and Mindset to Live Better*
*The Successful Spirit: Top Performers Share Secrets to a Winning Mindset*
*Winning Mindset: Elite Strategies for Peak Performance*
*Winner's Mindset: Peak Performance Strategies for Success*
*The AI Advantage: Thriving Within Civilization's Next Big Disruption*
*The AI Revolution: Thriving Within Civilization's Next Big Disruption*
*The AI Mindset: Thriving Within Civilization's Next Big Disruption*
*AI: Work Smarter and Live Better Within Civilization's Next Big Disruption*
*The Life Coach's Tool Kit, Vol. 1*
*The Life Coach's Tool Kit, Vol. 2*
*The Life Coach's Tool Kit, Vol. 3*
*Ordinary to Extraordinary*
*The Magical Lightness of Being*
*Explore.*

www.ingramcontent.com/pod-product-compliance
Lightning Source LLC
Chambersburg PA
CBHW062129020426
42335CB00013B/1155